~

DOWNHOME

~

For Sherry

DOWNHOME
Dispatches from Dixie

~

BOB DART

Southern Lion Books
Madison, Georgia

Published by
Southern Lion Books
Historical Publications
1280 Westminster Way
Madison, Georgia 30650
www.southernlionbooks.com

First Printing

Manufactured in the United States of America.

Library of Congress Control No. 2007942887
ISBN 978-0-9794203-3-7

The paper in this book meets the guidelines for permanence
and durability of the Committee on Production Guidelines
for Book Longevity of the Council on Library Resources.

Layout by Burt & Burt Studio
www.burtandburt.com

SOUTHERNERS

KATRINA

A SENSE OF PLACE

A MOONPIE MURDER AND OTHER MAYHEM

INDULGENCES

RUMINATIONS

JOURNEYS

Foreword

As a young reporter for the Atlanta Journal and Constitution, I found myself chatting with a Ku Klux Klansman one sweltering summer afternoon in downtown Decatur, Alabama.

I was covering racial confrontations that had been ignited by the case of Tommy Lee Hines, a retarded black man who had been convicted of raping a white woman. In the down time between two dueling protest marches, my curiosity compelled me to ask this avowed racist in full KKK regalia—tall, pointed hat and long-sleeved, ground-length robe and ax handle in his right hand—whether this outfit wasn't unbearably hot under such a merciless Southern sun.

He replied that it was surprisingly cool since the bright white material—which looked to be satin—reflected the sunlight. Besides, he confided, he was only wearing Bermuda shorts and a T-shirt underneath.

His eyes were covered by the sort of sunglasses that looked like mirrors from the outside looking in. I could see the reflection of my sunburned, sweaty face in the lens and wondered to myself, "Am I really having this conversation with this person in this place?"

I remember thinking "This is a surreal journalistic journey I'm beginning" as I seized upon the South as my beat. Three decades later, I still marvel at how strange and surprising my beloved home region can be when I head out to write about a Hurricane Katrina on the Gulf Coast or an asylum for psychotic parrots in rural North Carolina.

Covering a raccoon hunt, I have run through swamps at midnight that I would never venture into during daylight—chasing baying dogs and unseen quarry. "That's my ol' Blue," a hunter would proclaim, identifying his beloved hound by the baying. "Red's got him treed," someone else would drawl, conjuring up a vision of some cornered critter. Meanwhile, I was praying that water moccasins slept soundly.

Riding the caboose of the Santa Train, I've thrown Christmas gifts to children who gathered by the tracks winding through Appalachia. I've eaten fried alligator, drunk moonshine, heard heavenly four-part harmony of gospel music quartets in a high school football stadium and smelled decaying bodies of my fellow Southerners—all in pursuit of stories across Dixie.

Covering a Republican National Convention at Dallas, I went to the South Fork Ranch—home of TV's Ewing clan—and watched Dallas Cowboy cheerleaders handing yellow roses to African-American Republicans who were learning to dance the Cotton-eyed Joe. Right by the pool where Miss Ellie used to eat breakfast, these GOP folk were drinking long-necked Lone Star beers and praising Ronald Reagan. That was the same Republican convention where I saw Jerry Falwell wearing a ten-gallon hat and sitting astride a longhorn steer at the ranch of Bunker Hunt, who you might remember as the Texas billionaire who tried to corner the world's silver market.

At the Democratic National Convention in Atlanta, I found out just how bad an idea it was for lobbyists to host an outdoors brunch in the zoo in August. Oh well, the flies had a good time.

Then there was the trial of Doctor Nick, the physician accused of providing Elvis with the addictive pills that led to the death of the King of Rock 'n Roll. I stayed at the Peabody Hotel in Memphis. Legend has it that the Mississippi Delta begins in the lobby of the Peabody and ends on Catfish Row in Vicksburg.

In actuality at the Peabody, at eleven o'clock every morning, a family of ducks comes down the elevator from its penthouse home and marches across the carpet to the fountain in the lobby. They swim around there until about 5:00 P.M. when they march to the elevator and go up to the penthouse. The Peabody plays a Sousa march as the ducks waddle across the lobby.

Some days I would go over to Graceland and discuss the trial with devoted fans on pilgrimages to the home of Elvis. They thought lynching would be too lenient a sentence. Doctor Nick's real name is George C. Nichopoulas. A colleague from another paper who was also covering the trial ran into a fire hydrant while jogging in downtown Memphis one night. The next morning he hobbled to the front of the courtroom on crutches and asked if Dr. Nichopoulas would prescribe him some pain pills.

Doctor Nick appeared not to appreciate the irony and humor.

But y'all can see how I might find some interesting stuff to write about in the South as I've reported on the region for the Atlanta Journal and Constitution since 1976.

For more than twenty years, I've been based in Washington, D.C., as a national correspondent for Cox Newspapers, a chain of about twenty dailies that stretches from West Palm Beach, Florida, to Austin, Texas, to Dayton, Ohio. So, of course, I've written a slew of stories and been to a mess of places that aren't in the South.

I embedded with an Army infantry scout troop and went with them on the invasion of Iraq, for instance. Come to think of it though, I trained with them in Fort Hood, Texas, and rode in a Humvee driven by a good ol' boy from Tennessee. After a daylong odyssey that included a $350 cab fare and a waylaid train, I made it from Washington, D.C. into New York City on September 11, 2001, and reported from the smoldering stumps of the Twin Towers. I covered the Olympics in Barcelona and shared tea and scones with Newt Gingrich in a proper English hotel before writing about him debating an empty chair at Oxford University.

But those are other tales for other books.

As a six-generation son of the South, my favorite stories somehow usually involve collard greens or football or road kill or country music or kudzu or such. A colleague at the Atlanta Journal and Constitution once accused me of loving to write about "Moonpie Murders"—gory, Gothic tales that always involve some shocked, small-town Sunday School teacher saying, "Things like this just don't happen around here." I'll admit to knocking on the door of a house trailer in North Georgia where they had a poultry processing plant nearby. I needed to ask the fellow inside about suspicions that someone had killed his common-law wife and thrown her body in a pit of chicken beaks, feathers and innards to decompose.

He didn't want to talk about it.

Taken together, this collection of fifty-two of my favorite stories paints a colorful cultural portrait of thirty years in the South—a place that is ever changing but where, as the song says, "Old times there are not forgotten."

But I didn't write these as sociological studies. These are true-life yarns—some even about my kinfolks and native coastal Georgia, all about the sorts of people and places I grew up amongst and amidst and that I have appreciated since boyhood.

Some stories take place in spots even diehard Southerners may not know exist. A tiny Virginia island in the Chesapeake Bay that is so isolated the residents still speak in the Elizabethan English of the pre-Revolutionary War colonists. A giant, high-tech hearing aid in Appalachia that is listening for voices from outer space. Fields of dreams in the Shenandoah Valley where college baseball players hone their talents and learn the lessons of life. The cab of a big-rig rumbling across the South with a philosopher shifting gears behind the wheel.

I only hope folks enjoy reading them as much as I enjoyed going out and reporting them and then sitting down and writing them.

Bob Dart
Vienna, Virginia
January 1, 2008

ROOTS

The author on the porch on St. Simons Island in 1996   *Photo by Sherry Dart*

Porch Swings

The neighbors laugh when they see the kids and me all bundled up in the dead of winter but still sitting on the front porch swing.

Now that the dogwoods are blooming on our street and the yards are ablaze with azaleas, the creaking of the chain is almost continuous. I figure that the porch swing is one of the few links between my Yankee offspring and their roots in the red clay of Georgia.

Historically and geographically, Fairfax County, Virginia, can be considered part of Dixie. But culturally, it's now part of the Washington megalopolis and is about as Southern as the microwaved bagels my children eat for breakfast. They grimace at grits, of course, and giggle indulgently at their parents' drawls.

But they love sitting in our front porch swing as much as my brothers and I loved swinging on the porch at our granddaddy's farmhouse in Jeff Davis County, Georgia.

Even across the true South, there are fewer porch swings nowadays. Folks once sat on them to shell butterbeans or gossip with the neighbors or entertain their suitors. Barefoot children swung impatiently on the porch as they waited for the dew to dry so they could run through the grass. Wrinkled, white-haired couples swung away their sunset years.

But then air conditioning and television came along, and the swings increasingly hung still and silent. Builders even stopped putting porches on houses, or they built pitiful little prop porches that were more of an architectural illusion than a place to sit.

Our house is nearly a century old and came with a porch swing. I was sold before the real estate agent took me through the front door.

Swings and rocking chairs have always been the favored furniture of front porches, rhythmic movement being strangely conducive to comfort and conversation. For, as the Encyclopedia of Southern Culture confirms, the porch's "most important ongoing use is to transmit folklore."

That's what happens in our swing.

The children have endured hundreds of "three little boy stories" about their dad and his two brothers and their adventures growing up in the South of the 1950s and '60s. And I've enjoyed almost daily updates on the advances of Jennifer and Rob through elementary school and into adolescence.

Inside the house, the pursuits tend toward the solitary—TV, Nintendo, homework. Outside, together on the swing, we've read aloud "To Kill a Mockingbird" and "Huckleberry Finn" as well as snippets from Mad magazine and Teen.

We've swung a million miles, whiled away too many hours to count. From my memories, they've learned where our family came from. From their shared thoughts and dreams, I'm learning where it's headed in the next generation.

That's why God made porch swings.

Family Reunion

Walter Clements, a curly-haired, blue-eyed farm boy from Telfair County, Georgia, courts and marries Emmy Pickren from the crossroads community of Snipesville. This wooing and winning occurs some twenty odd years after the Civil War. Her daddy gives them 100 acres of woodland in Jeff Davis County to clear and cultivate and Emmy is soon with child.

But Emmy dies giving birth to a daughter named Fannie. After a time of mourning, Walter takes Emmy's younger sister, Clara Pickren, as his new wife. The sharp-tongued daughter of a schoolmarm, Clara rears her niece and bears seven children of her own by Walter. They all live in a little house in a cornfield and the children learn early that the business end of a hoe fits their hands right well.

Hoover's Depression is hard upon Georgia when Walter dies. He leaves his offspring little but their share of the farm and the intimate knowledge of the back end of a mule that comes from steering a plow.

The brothers and sisters marry young. Charlie weds a Douglas. Ida becomes an Austin. Jake takes a wife named Kate while his sister, Kate, marries a lanky, soft-spoken fellow named Hobson Smith. Bob marries Stella Lamb when she is but fifteen and he is not much older. Roselene, the baby, hitches up with a banjo playing turpentine man named McCall.

Times are hard and most of the family stays close to the land. Bob hires out as a one-mule sharecropper and saves up and buys a place of his own. Buddy goes into the service. Jake drives a school bus and opens a store. The McCalls prosper at several ventures. The men hunt and fish and farm. The women cook and clean and have babies. It all ages them beyond their years.

Even in a county where Baptists and bootleggers keep hard liquor outlawed, some of the brothers take more than an occasional nip. Their redemption is prayed for by the siblings that don't. Ida drops dead of a heart attack in a tobacco warehouse when she is but forty. Bob's wife dies in childbirth, leaving him three daughters to finish raising. A new generation of cousins scrap and study at Excelsior School, the nine-grade schoolhouse that sits across from Sinclair's Grocery. For decades, those are the only structures in Snipesville.

There are family fish fries by the Ocmulgee River and Sunday dinners on the ground at Mount Pleasant Baptist Church.

World War II comes and several of the boys are called up. Some of the girls as well as the boys find good-paying jobs in shipyards and defense plants. They find spouses elsewhere. After V-E and V-J Days, some of the boys come back with a whiff of a wider world and a yen for an easier life. By 1952, when Granny Clara Clements is lowered into the red clay to rest beside Walter, cousins are scattered like birdshot—some to raise citified children who know little of the little house in the cornfield.

~

Nearly three decades had passed since the kindred gathered to mourn Clara Clements' passing when a great-granddaughter down in Miami got the notion to reassemble the whole clan.

The first effort got limp reception. Rural relatives had tobacco to pick. Urban ones got lost looking for the right bend in the Ocmulgee.

But the Clementses can be stubborn. The following summer they have a go at another reunion. This time it's on a Sunday, after church, at a park by a highway that could be found even by the cross-eyed hound that Charlie once sold Jake. This time, aging mamas successfully shamed grown children who had previously balked at bringing their own off-spring to meet third cousins from God Knows Where. Grandmas pointed out that grandpas don't live forever. So it came to pass that a couple of hundred of the descendants of Walter and Clara Clements came to gather under a wooden pavilion at General Coffee State Park near Douglas, Georgia, to eat a lot and talk a little with their distant kin.

~

There is not much about this family gathering, of course, to distinguish it from scores of others held across the South every summer.

Except this commentator showed up with his brood of Clements descendants.

"You must be one of Walter Green Austin's boys."

"No ma'am. I'm Opal's oldest son, Bob."

"Well, you don't favor her much do you? That your son you've got there? Fine looking boy. Must take after his mama."

"Yes ma'am."

Naturally the older kin who had shared their childhoods take up talking where they left off years ago. They recall hard days in cotton fields and easy ones beside fish ponds. They laugh about dressing up Coke bottles in scraps of clothing because there was no money to buy dolls. Of the eight children of Walter Clements, only Roselene and Buddy are living. And Buddy doesn't come. But many of the children of those Clements brothers and sisters are there. And a slew of their children show up from across several states. They bring their own young'uns—the great-great-grandchildren in this lineage.

This youngest set is clamoring to eat long before the appointed hour of 1:00 P.M. Roy and Homer have spent much of the previous day and night barbecuing a young hog and an old deer. The aroma of this smoked meat convinces even the most sophisticated of the teenage cousins that coming here wasn't such a bad idea after all.

The various factions begin arriving in earnest about noon. Some men wear caps that advertise farm implements while the caps of others identify golf clubs. Some sport polo players on the breast of the shirts, others keep a plug of tobacco in their breast pockets. One of Aunt

Roselene's grandsons saunters up in a straw cowboy hat with a good-looking girl in short shorts on his arm. Three sisters from south Florida wear matching green t-shirts that chronicle the event: "Clements Family Reunion '80." A long-haired college girl strums a guitar and somebody says she is a Sigma Nu sweetheart on her campus. Kids in cut-off jeans and football jerseys scamper through the pines to the nearby pool and playground.

There's a good representation, everyone agrees. Some of Uncle Charlie's people are here. And Aunt Fannie's. Bob Clements was killed more than a decade earlier when his tractor turned over as he drove across the dam between a fish pond and branch. But all three of his schoolteacher daughters—Opal, Pat and Dorothy—are there, as are their children and grandchildren. A fair-sized delegation of Austins has come from Fernandina Beach. Aunt Kate's middle son had been shot dead in an argument with a man he had known all his life, but her other sons, Roy and Ernest, are there with wives and offspring.

The women set to work upon arrival, pulling tables together to form a long serving place and arranging the food in logical order. In their previews, the cooks tend to degrade the feast they are busily spreading.

"I'm afraid that corn on the cob will be hard. We picked it mighty late in the season."

"Well, I don't know what happened to make that cake fall. I'm afraid it won't be fitten to eat."

Meanwhile, most of the men gather in distinct little clumps to await dinner. The talk among some runs to the crops and the dryness of the summer. In the midday heat, others are already missing their air conditioners and TVs back home. In-laws who wouldn't know a Clements from Adam, save the one they married, fend for themselves with introductions. There is a general time of catching up on lost years. Vance, Roselene's son, has been elected a Jeff Davis County commissioner. Opal's boy, Bill, came home from Alaska with a wife and is running a seafood plant on St. Simons Island. Ernest's wife, Nancy, taught herself to play the organ and accompanies the hymns at their church. Dorothy's husband is a pharmacist with the busiest drug store in Pearson.

Small talk amongst fifth cousins to an acquaintance tends to run thin, though. Everyone is ready to eat when one of Walter Clements' grandsons bangs a ladle against a pot lid to call them all to the tables beneath a pavilion.

Brother James Laquire of the Macedonia Church of God gives lengthy thanks for the bountiful food and family now assembled. The amens are still echoing as folks start down the long line to load their plates. There's fried chicken, home-cured ham, smoked turkey, roast beef and the aforementioned barbecue. And dressing, biscuits, squash, lady-finger peas, collard greens and other fresh vegetables, an assortment of casseroles, homemade pickles and relishes, potato salad, deviled eggs, chicken and dumplings, sliced tomatoes and cucumbers, Brunswick stew and a myriad of other dishes regretfully neglected because of the necessity of keeping the line moving. There are well placed Igloo coolers of iced sweet tea and a separate table of cakes, pies and custards.

Despite the dire predictions of some of the chefs, the food is eaten with enthusiasm and dispatch and without discrimination. There are no speeches to interrupt the second helpings or the thirds. Oratory is not a Clements' trait.

It's not long before folks are pushing back their chairs from the tables. The women gossip as they clean up. The children run off to play some more. The men seek out the scant shade of jack pines where they whittle and smoke and chew. There's a recalling of good dogs and bad women.

Homer describes again the 200-pound pumpkin that he grew this year.

"Biggest in the history of Jeff Davis County. I got in the pickup and carried pieces to everyone I know and still had some left over."

Families are already loading up and heading out when a photographer tries to arrange a group shot of the whole bunch. Other problems have set in. The babies are crying for their naps. The full-bellied old men are ready to lie down on a couch. Children are tired and cross and mamas are in no mood for sass. Daddies dread the long drives home

The farewell is as familiar as the family, as old as the region itself.

Y'all come see us now.

A Football Weekend at Ole Miss

The weekend began shortly after noon on Thursday in Business Ethics class. Richard Johnson turned to Brad Huff, his Phi Delta Theta fraternity brother, and said "Let's go to the line."

And off they went before the prof could declare their departure an asset or a liability.

It's a traditional trip. Ole Miss boys have suffered the vagaries of Lafayette County liquor laws for generations. The current quirk is that cold beer can't be sold for take-out. Young thirst won't wait for a warm six-pack to chill. So Richard and Brad headed to the county line. Just on the other side, more lenient laws prevail and establishments like Pete's One-Stop provide ice-cold beer ready to be taken back to Oxford.

Tradition is an important part of life here in the land of magnolias and Faulkner and bourbon and catfish and the Ole Miss Rebels. For the two Phi Delts and scores of other students, the trip to the line is ritualistic and as much a part of a football weekend as the pep rally, singing of "Dixie," happy hours at the bars off the Square, tailgating in the Grove, Fraternity Row parties and the game itself.

Ole Miss plays the University of Georgia here on Saturday. The game is important to both teams. But it is only a game. Something deeper surrounds it. Something akin to heritage. A Southern subculture perhaps. It's a way of life that has defied change for decades and will be here long after the score on Saturday is forgotten.

"The past is not dead," said William Faulkner, who understood this hallowed, haunted place like no other. "In fact, it is not even past."

For generations, the fraternity boys of Ole Miss have had first names like last names. At the Sigma Alpha Epsilon house—where Bill Faulkner was a brother—there's Hayes Dent, Walker Jones and Coleman Conner. Crawford Dean and Newell Turner are Kappa Alphas. The mingling of family names illustrates the continuity of this place. Like the big river itself, time rolls on slowly here.

The turbulence of the late 1960s and early 1970s—when anti-Vietnam War protests and flower-power politics drastically changed other campuses—caused barely a ripple at Ole Miss.

"We certainly had a minimum of those who wished to experiment and by the time they felt free to do so, the fashion had changed anyway," said Frank Moak, the dean of students and a 1948 Ole Miss grad.

One of the biggest protests of the Sixties came over beer laws in Oxford when students marched on the mayor's house.

Of course, racial integration came hard here.

In 1962, James Meredith became the first black student at Ole Miss. It took federal troops to get him enrolled. But Ross Barnett—the segregationist governor who fought to keep out Meredith and other African-Americans—is just a name in a history book to Ole Miss students now. From kindergarten through high school, most attended racially integrated schools. Black and white, they practice a sort of in-bred Southern courtesy—habitually saying "Yes ma'am" and "Yes sir" and remembering from Sunday School the "Golden Rule" of "Do unto others . . ."

Social conservatism has always been fashionable here.

Until the mid-1960s, there was a dress code at Ole Miss. Estella G. Hefley, long-time dean of women, enforced the standards for co-eds. A girl wearing gym shorts on campus, for instance, would have to wear a raincoat over them.

Appearance is still important. The beauty of Ole Miss girls is legendary and they make up conscientiously to attend class.

"And the boys dress up more than the girls do," said Karlen Goldman, a blonde Phi Mu from Meridian.

As in most things here, there is order to courtship. "Dropped, pinned, then engaged," said Karlen, explaining the progression.

"Dropped" is the wearing of a boyfriend's fraternity lavaliere. "Pinned" means the relationship is more serious—"engaged to be engaged"—and she wears his fraternity pin. "Engaged" is sometimes still equated with co-ed collegiate success.

The student newspaper, The Daily Mississippian, has a column called "The Hitching Post" that records these relationships.

"Sure, I want to graduate and find some rich guy to marry," admitted Karlen, who is bright enough to survive as an accounting major. "I don't want to go to work."

"But it looks like I'll have to," she sighed. She graduates in December and laughingly held up a bare ring finger on her left hand.

Some sorority girls dispute the stereotypes.

"People think of Ole Miss girls as made-up Southern belles who spend all their time rolling their hair. But I don't think we're like that at all," protested Melissa Flood, a Tri Delt. "And people say Ole Miss girls are snotty and stuck up. That's not true at all."

But nobody goes as far to say that dating is not important on an autumn weekend.

"It's bad if you don't have a date for a home football game," said Karlen. "Especially when you're a freshman. Then you think you just have to have one."

Now that she's a senior and older than most of the boys on campus, she conceded, it doesn't seem so important. However, she does have a date for the Georgia game.

Pledges are "fixed up" with blind dates—with unpredictable results.

Elizabeth Weatherly, a Tri Delt, laughed about a bad experience after being "fixed up" with a Sigma Chi pledge.

"He was a pine tree," she recalled. "He just stood there all night. I finally left him."

Of course, it's vital to wear the right clothes to the game and the pre- and-post game gatherings in the Grove. For boys, it's a heavily starched, Oxford cloth, button-down collared, long-sleeved shirt and a tie. Trousers are crisply creased khakis. Laundries thrive in Oxford. Often blazers are worn to games even under the Mississippi sun, for they provide cover for pocket flasks of Jim Beam or Jack Daniels. Bass Weejuns are still the favored male footwear.

Girls wear J. G. Hook skirts, Oxford-cloth shirts and blazers. Or pretty, light-weight dresses. Strands of pearls are always appropriate. Their shoes are Pappagallos or Capezio. Their hair is perfect.

Ole Miss and Oxford are about the same size, both with populations just over 9,000. City and campus merge unnoticeably along University Avenue. There's never been much town and gown conflict.

"In the state, we get the cream of the crop. Good kids," said John Leslie, mayor of Oxford and proprietor of the drugstore across from the Lafayette County Courthouse. "They get drunk, sure, but you never see any rough stuff. . . . And we've got the best-looking girls in the country. No doubt about it."

Football weekends highlight the social calendar for both campus and town. By Thursday afternoon before a Saturday game, college boys and girls are cruising in cars—drinking beer and checking each other out. By the Oxford Square, the Warehouse and the Gin are packed with happy hour celebrants. There is a pep rally on Thursday night and a concert afterward.

Fridays feature another packed happy hour at the Warehouse and the Gin—favored bars for students. That night, there are open parties along Fraternity Row, with thousands of students wandering and drinking and stopping to dance to a score of bands playing on lawns and in party basements.

At eleven o'clock on Friday night, though, pick-up trucks stocked with party provisions make their way to the Grove, a ten-acre stand of oak, elm and magnolia near Hemingway Stadium (which was named for an Ole Miss law professor, not the author).

At midnight, university police let in those responsible for preparation. They rush to familiar spots and set up brightly colored tents, tables, chairs, coolers, barbecue smokers, flags and, sometimes, even chandeliers. By the wee hours of Saturday morning, the serious partying has begun.

"The glory of the Grove is legend at all of Ole Miss's rival schools in the Southeastern Conference and beyond," the New York Times itself proclaimed. "It is the mother and mistress of outdoor ritual mayhem."

Alumni and students mingle for hours amid a heady mix of gossip, flirtation, Bloody Marys, champagne cocktails, deviled eggs, pimento cheese, bourbon and Coke, shared school spirit, fried chicken and to-die-for fashion. Decades fade away on Saturdays in the Grove.

David G. Sansing, a professor emeritus at Ole Miss who has written a history of the university, described the significance to the New York Times.

"Your college days are the fondest years of your life, and those memories of those years grow rosier as time recedes," he explained. "When these alumni come back and walk through that grove, they're not just walking over land—ground—they're walking back through time."

Several hours before kick-off, the Ole Miss players take the "Rebel Walk" through the grove to the stadium. They are cheered with gusto and slap hands with partiers who line up along their route—the brick Walk of Champions.

Order is maintained by the Grove Society, an alumni group that sets schedules and establishes rules for real estate. Demand always exceeds supply for prime party plots.

In this Ole Miss thicket, which has become a community of tents, a chant regularly rings out.

"Hotty Toddy, Gawd Almighty, Who the hell are we? Flim Flam. Bim Bam. Ole Miss, by damn!"

By the thousands, folks meander from tent to tent—with these social shelters often marked by names of families, fraternities, sororities or towns. Elaborate meals begin with Saturday breakfast and continue to a pre-game brunch and post-game dinner.

Political deals are made in the Grove. Marriages come together and break apart. Lifetime bonds of friendship are forged and then renewed autumn after autumn. Mississippi is a small place really—sometimes more of a club than a state, according to Willie Morris, at times an Ole Miss writer in residence.

The score of a football game is not the important part of these weekends. Alumni and students alike are sad when Sunday afternoons arrive.

"It's like a little bubble here," said Annette Rand, an Ole Miss student from Gulfport. "It's not the real world at all."

Songs of the Sapelo

This here's the Ballad of Vic Waters. Ol' Vic is a red-bearded, shrimp-eating, guitar-picking poet who lives by a bend in the Sapelo River and chronicles the goings-on of McIntosh County, a marshy, mysterious place down on the Georgia coast.

There was the time, for instance, when Sheriff Tom Poppell and a band of federal drug enforcement agents got tangled up in The Saga of the Great Sapelo Pot Bust of 1975. Here's how Vic describes it:

There was a full moon shining on the river when the boat came in with the goods.

The high sheriff was hiding in the marsh grass, while the customs men waited in the woods.

The sheriff didn't know about the customs men and the customs men didn't know about no sheriff…

When the lights came on over the water, it nearly scared everybody to death.

Sheriff Poppell—a lawman of longevity and notoriety—died in 1979. But there is still considerable discussion in McIntosh County on how he happened to be there when the dope smugglers landed and the feds sprang their secret sting. No matter, he joined in the bust. And Vic Waters had himself another epic.

He sings these stories, by the way, at a cement block bar called the Oyster Shucker that's located beneath a shade oak and beside a black-top road leading off state Highway 99 between Eulonia and Valona.

"I opened it so I would have a place to play," Vic explained. Patrons of the art of rhymes and rhythms drive over from Shellman's Bluff and St. Simons and Midway and Brunswick to hear him sing and to handle a few long-necked bottles of Bud. It ain't easy to find his place.

"I don't get much drop-in-trade." allowed Waters. "Except for the people who stop in after eating seafood up the road at the Buccaneer Club."

Even inlanders have heard of the Buccaneer, which was famous for serving big, fresh, fried mounds of the river's bounty. But then the Buccaneer burned down.

~

Vic Waters was born thirty-eight years ago in this low country of tide-water rivers and marsh grass prairies and hard-living fishermen. As a boy, he played with the fiddlers that scurry over the mud flats at low tide. He crabbed off the docks that extend from most back yards. He fished in the inlets and explored Blackbeard's Island, where the famed pirate would rest after plundering.

His daddy was a truck driver who pulled off one day when Vic was young and didn't come back. His mama was a waitress at a Sapelo River seafood restaurant. "They sold bait and rented boats there during the week and held square dances on Saturday nights," he recalled.

He learned to pick and sing early, and he grew up wise and obser-vant. He knew of the pecan stands on U.S. 17 where Yankee tourists would stop for gas or souvenirs and be lured into crooked games of chance. When the visitors took their complaints to Sheriff Poppell, he informed them that gambling was illegal in McIntosh County so filing charges would land them in jail. Vic knew of the truck stop where long-distance drivers and adolescent boys could rent love or something akin to it. He heard tales of shrimper fights at The Crows Nest Bar and legends of deadly men like Sapelo River Red:

"His skin was black as an eight ball and his hair was fiery red.
They said he killed a man in Jacksonville, put a crowbar up side of his
head . . .
'Course nobody worries about Red no more.
He's dead and that's all she wrote.
Lightning danced across the marsh grass and fried him in his boat."

There is only one traffic light in McIntosh County. It's a slow-paced place. But it's hard. Centuries ago, pirates docked here and some folks say their lineage lingers. After high school, Vic took his guitar and hit the road, headed to musical fame and fortune. He played beer joints and he sold used cars. A dozen years later—then thirty years old with a wife and two sons—he was ready to come home:

"Born and raised on the Sapelo River, I left to get some schooling.
But now I'm back and I realize I'm the only one I was fooling."

He had a twelve-piece rhythm-and-blues band back then, but figured that he would have to make it as a solo act to survive in McIntosh County. His return engagement was as a replacement for an organ player from Ludowici who had been grinding out funeral music to entertain customers at David Hornsby's cocktail lounge in Eulonia.

Vic Waters was back to stay.

~

He lives with his wife and sons in a house with a back porch that overlooks the river and marshes. There are rocking chairs and a swing on the porch. His flower beds are bordered by conch shells. Shrimp boats tie up next door. There's a hammock hung on the Waters' dock and a fishing boat tied beneath a tin shed. The house is down a dirt road from where he grew up. He had wanted to buy it for years.

"One morning the owner called me and told me, 'I've been saved,' and that he was going to Shreveport, Louisiana, to study evangelism. He asked me if I still wanted to buy the house," Vic said. "I said 'Bingo, praise the Lord'."

He remodeled the house himself, doing the carpentry and masonry with help from an out-of-work shrimper.

Of course, Vic Waters is not without fame. He has two record albums that sell steadily between Savannah and St. Mary's. He's going to Nashville someday to cut another.

"Shoot, on October 21, 1980, I did the Grand Ole Opry. I followed George Jones," said Vic. "He killed 'em. I got a picture to show my grandchildren one day."

He's done big concerts. It hasn't always gone over well. "It's hard as hell to do a single in front of a bunch of stoned Lynyrd Skynyrd freaks."

Now, he mostly stays around McIntosh County, doing the things he's always done. He laments some of the changes he sees. The law padlocked the gyp joints on U.S. 17 long ago, for instance, and the general store where the bus once stopped has closed.

"When the Greyhound stops to let him off, it won't seem like home no more.

They closed down all the pecan shops and they tore down Jenkins Store

. . .

It was a mighty sad day for Sapelo Bay when they tore down Jenkins Store."

His neighbors can visit his bar only occasionally. "Shrimp fishermen don't spend much money in bars," he explained. "They get 'em a jug and take it back on the boat 'cause they got to get up at 3 A.M."

His red beard is flecked with gray now, but he still wears t-shirts and jeans. He has his family and he has his river and he has his songs. Vic Waters knows there is something to be said for living your life like you want:

"Sapelo River, take me home. Let me fish you one more time. Sapelo River, take me home. You are a friend of mine."

A Family Saga in Black and White

The bones of Cyrus Dart rest beneath the grayish-green waters off this blessed barrier isle.

My great-great-great-grandfather was a medical doctor and the quarantine officer for the port in the decades following the American Revolution. In 1817, he drowned at the age of fifty-three when his rowboat capsized on the way to inspect a ship's crew for communicable diseases. He was accompanied by his young son, Urbanus, who managed to swim safely ashore. Otherwise, I would not be here to chronicle this saga of a Southern family in black and white.

Cyrus could not have imagined the diversity of descendants who gathered here on Patriot's Day to honor the patriarch of Dixie's branch of the Dart family tree.

Folks say there is a sense of place in the soul of Southern families.

For me, that sense of place centers on Glynn County, the home of my forebears and site of the marshes and beaches where I grew up. But there are as many such home places as there are multi-hued families throughout the South, where people different in many ways can come together to explore their shared ancestry.

In this region so long troubled by issues of race, many of us really are brothers and sisters under our skins.

Born and reared in Connecticut, Cyrus came to Georgia after serving as an underage private in the Revolutionary Army and then completing his medical studies. Since his body was never recovered from the Atlantic, it would be two centuries before a marker honoring his military service would be placed beside the grave of his wife, the former Ann Harris of St. Simons. She is buried on the grounds of Christ Church near the island's historic Fort Frederica, which dates to the settlement of the colony of Georgia by General James Oglethorpe.

At a ceremony organized by the Georgia Society of the Sons of the American Revolution, descendants of Cyrus Dart and three other Revolutionary War soldiers gathered beneath the live oaks on a spring morning. We shooed away sand gnats and hugged our distant kin.

Amongst my family, there were black cousins from Maryland and New Jersey and Brunswick, which is just across the marshes. There were white cousins from Chicago and Miami and Tennessee and Jesup, which is forty miles through piney woods on U.S. 341.

Many knew each other only by the lapel markers we wore bearing an American flag and the words "Cyrus Dart."

"I was actually a little nervous," said Rena Page, thirty, an African-American graphic designer from Jessup, Maryland. Her lineage to Cyrus goes through one of his grandsons—although there is some dispute as to which son of Urbanus it was.

The death certificates for Earl and Roland Dart—biracial brothers who started at least one branch of the family tree—list their father as "Bonnie Dart." That could be Urbanus Dart, Jr. who was known as Barney Dart.

The African-American Darts know their ancestor was also a "Judge Dart" but there were two "Judge Darts" in this generation—Urbanus Jr. "Barney" Dart and his brother Horace Dart. Both fought for the Confederacy in the Civil War.

There is no doubt, though, that Earl and Roland were grandsons of Cyrus Dart, the Revolutionary War veteran honored at the ceremony that brought together his descendants.

"I didn't know what the reaction would be. I didn't know who knew. I've always known. The older generation kept it alive for us," said Rena, an Army Reservist and owner of Tusk Grafx. Her grandmother, Norene Dart Page, seventy-nine, grew up in Brunswick but moved to Newark, New Jersey in 1950. Norene Dart Page is the daughter of Earl Dart. Roland Dart was her uncle.

"The boys were raised by a woman named Emma. We never knew who their mother was. I wish I did," said Norene. "My Uncle Roland told me that, during that time, some of the Darts had wanted the boys' names changed. But someone in authority in the family said, 'A Dart is a Dart whether he is black or white'."

Growing up in Brunswick during the era of segregation, I always knew there were black Darts and white Darts in our town and that we were somehow connected. But I was more concerned with football and the beach and girls than with genealogy.

As a child, I once asked my mother about some Darts in the Glynn County phone book with first names that I didn't recognize. She said they were descendants of slaves who had taken the family name after being freed.

Since some of my ancestors were slave owners, that was true as far as it went. But we were also blood kin, some born of relationships that came long after the Civil War.

In Brunswick, the races "didn't mingle much back then," said Norene. She remembers her sister meeting a white woman at the health department once and being asked her name. "My sister said 'Ethel Dart.' And the white woman said, 'My name is Ethel Dart, too'."

I asked Rena if her side of the family bore a grudge from those times.

"We have no resentment at all," she said. "I loved the ceremony and I was determined to go."

There were family tales to share.

By the time Urbanus, the son who swam to shore when Cyrus drowned, reached manhood, the town of Brunswick had largely been deserted. Through some legal maneuvering, he gained ownership of much of the property and promoted the re-establishment of the community. He donated the land upon which most of the town's churches were built and still stand. He also served in the state Legislature.

The Georgia poet Sidney Lanier wrote his classic ode "The Marshes of Glynn" while sitting beneath an oak tree in the front yard of my great-grandfather, the first William Robert Dart. The tree is now memorialized as "Lanier's Oak" and the Victorian house is home to the Brunswick-Glynn County Chamber of Commerce.

There is also a story about Aretha Dart, Norene's sister, going to court before yet another Judge Dart after a confrontation with a white woman who was visiting Brunswick from Valdosta during the Jim Crow era. Aretha was the cousin of this Judge, although he showed no official recognition.

The visiting white woman "was calling my sister names," said Norene. Judge Dart told her to stop.

"Then he told my sister to look away when she passed the woman's house," recalled Norene. "And he told the white woman that the sooner she could go back to Valdosta, the better."

~

CELEBRITIES
OF SORTS

~

Ol' Cooter   Photo by Rick McKay

Junior Samples

To get to Junior's house, you turn off Setting Down Road onto an uphill dirt driveway marked "Jr S Drive." There's a sign nailed to a telephone pole that warns: "Private. A Man's Home is His Castle. Please. Entry by Invitation Only."

But, there really isn't much security—considering that this is the home of Junior Samples, star of "Hee Haw" and a genuine TV personality.

The personality himself answers the door, looking less than robust. Junior just got out of the hospital.

"I'm some better now," he allowed, easing his posterior into a porch swing. "I was on the verge of having a heart attack."

His doctor had called it a hardening of the arteries. Serious enough to give a man a glimpse of his own mortality, enough to make him reflect on his life up to then. That reflection, in the case of "Hee Haw's" bountiful bumbler, covers considerable territory.

"When I look back over it, it's a wonder I made it through alive," he admits. "I've done things a man couldn't do twice in his life."

To start with, Junior Samples found fame—and some riches—partly because he got drunk enough one time to tell a whopping fish tale to a city fellow. Junior claimed to have caught the world's biggest bass.

Before that, he had lived hard with his wife and six children in a three-room, $25-a-month shack near the waterworks outside this little town in North Georgia.

"I did about anything to make a dollar," he recalled.

Junior was a sawmill man sometimes. Other times he was a pulp woodsman or a carpenter or a moonshiner. "I made liquor in every branch in Forsyth County and in a few chicken coops, too," he said.

Mostly though, Junior was that fun-loving breed of Southerner called a "good ol' boy" by his buddies but called "no 'count" by their wives.

"My old lady was working. Making a living. The neighbors all tended to my business so I just hunted and fished mostly," he recalled. "That's the way it should have been, too. Like the Indians."

Then, in 1967, an official from the Georgia Game and Fish Commission heard a radio report that one Junior Samples had caught a world record bass. Actually Junior's brother, Monroe, had found the fish—a saltwater grouper—on the side of a highway. Apparently, it had been tossed out by a fisherman passing through Forsyth County on his way home from the coast. Junior cut off the fish's head and proclaimed the body was a bass he had caught.

When the Game and Fish fellow reached Forsyth County, he found Junior sitting on his front porch nipping at his second pint of the day.

"He said he come up after a story about the fish. I didn't think he was going to leave so I just went and drunk me another drink and told him I'd tell him one."

What followed was one of those only-in-America success stories.

Junior's fish story was taped. Although it was quickly exposed as a hoax, the telling was so funny that a record was made in Nashville. Junior became a comedian, working little clubs across the South and eventually performing at the Grand Ole Opry. He said things funny more than he said funny things.

"But I didn't get on 'Hee Haw' because of that fish story," he stressed. "I had to take a test for it like everyone else."

That was in 1969. The new "Hee Haw" program—sort of a corn-pone version of "Laugh-In"—offered to pay him "either $73 or $93 to audition." So he went to Nashville.

A writer gave him a card with his lines to read. Junior said he couldn't.

"I told them to give me some four-letter words to read. They said I couldn't say no dirty words on TV but I told them I meant words like 'they' or 'what.' I could read those words but not the big ones on that card."

Samples said the writer told him to just read what he thought the words on the card were. "I did and it just broke him up."

A star was born.

Shortly thereafter, Junior Samples moved his family to the nice brick house off Setting Down Road and settled into the good life. Nowadays, he goes to Nashville twice a year—for about two weeks each trip—to tape "Hee Haw." For those four weeks work, which consists mostly of standing in a fake cornfield, wearing bib overalls and a t-shirt, and flubbing lines on-camera, he is paid about $30,000.

"I think the Lord done it," he said.

~

There was a time when Grace Samples would load the dinner table with fried chicken and pork chops, collard greens and ham hocks, cornbread and light bread, okra and tomatoes, sweet potato pie and whatever else her husband hankered for that noon. But Junior has to watch what he eats now.

"Oh hell yes, I'm on a diet. Salad. Lettuce. Cabbage. Boiled weeds of any kind but she can't put grease in with them for flavor."

"It ain't no two or three day thing. I've got to stay on it."

It's the worst at breakfast when he used to eat four or five eggs, a few biscuits and a slab of salty country ham. But he has lost twenty-five pounds—from 300 pounds down to 275.

But that's small consolation to a man who takes pleasure in food. One of the treasures that his TV money provided was a deep freezer that he stocked with game, fish and vegetables. His missing front teeth never slowed him down at the table either, he recalled.

"I have to go after an apple different. It hindered me some eating corn on the cob, too. It looks like it went through a sheller half way when I get through with it."

He had the front teeth pulled back when he was having some troubles with women. Then his wife made him start dipping snuff, too, he said, as another ploy to keep away female rivals.

"It must have worked 'cause they don't bother me much now," he said.

Even before his hospital stay, Junior said he had stopped his drinking.

"I ain't drank a drop of nothing in six years except maybe a sip of champagne on a plane or something. It got to where it hurt me. I don't like pain and if I know what's doing it, I'm going to stop.

"It's like the time I got locked up for being drunk in Cumming when I was about eighteen. I ain't been back to Cumming drunk since."

There was some debate about that several years back.

In 1973, Junior and his son, Emory Junior Samples, who was twenty-five at the time, were arrested when they went to the Forsyth County Jail after midnight to bail out Junior's business manager. The manager had been charged with driving under the influence. At the jail, Junior got into an altercation with a deputy and was charged with public drunkenness.

But the "Hee Haw" star was acquitted after taking the stand at his trial—wearing bib overalls and a yellow T-shirt—and swearing "I hadn't drank one drop."

He'd been dipping snuff at the time, Junior testified, and you can't drink and dip at the same time because snuff is too hard to get out of your mouth when it's time for another drink.

Fame never went to Junior's head, his neighbors say.

"He still comes in here between five and six o'clock most mornings to talk," said the fellow by the cold drink box at the Lake Lanier Sporting Goods bait shop.

But the TV star does have the words "Hee Haw" spelled out in dimes embedded in the concrete on his carport.

The dimes "are so people can walk on money when they come to see me," he explained. But now some have been pried up and carried off "by the danged souvenir hunters."

～

Junior Samples died of a heart attack on November 13, 1983, at fifty.

Champaign, Illinois, 1985

Willie's Woodstock

The bountiful prairie cornfields run smack into the city limits of the college community that is hosting what folks hereabouts have dubbed
"Willie's Woodstock."

The deep black earth of central Illinois is as fertile as any on the continent and bumper crops await harvest in the September heat. But record
yields are a bitter blessing when it costs a farmer more to grow his corn
than the market will pay for it.

That's why ol' Willie has summoned the stars of American music to
the heartland.

Willie, of course, is Willie Nelson, the red-haired guitar picker who
put together this Farm Aid Concert and promises to pull off such
musical gatherings every year until the nation's family farmers are eco-
nomically secure.

"I guess this is my first crusade," allows Nelson. "I have friends all
over Texas who are farmers and they tell me the situation is serious.
People are losing their homes and land through no fault of their own.
There seems to be an injustice there somewhere."

Not since the legendary, musically magical gathering in a meadow in
upstate New York—the event that would become a cultural milestone in
the nation's history—has there been such an assembly of singing talent
from all genres. At times, the stage set up on the Fighting Illini football
field became a rockabilly paradise with Johnny Cash, Waylon Jennings,

Roy Orbison and Kris Kristofferson joining voices. Backed by Tom Petty and the Heartbreakers, Bob Dylan sang "I Ain't Gonna Work on Maggie's Farm No More." Billy Joel—after bragging about growing up next to a potato farm on Long Island—sang in a trio with Bonnie Raitt and Daryl Hall. Sammy Hagar sang "I Can't Drive 55" and performed for the first time with Van Halen as the replacement for departed lead singer David Lee Roth.

After finishing their set, the bandsmen of Bon Jovi were asked what a bunch of rockers from New Jersey knew about farming.

"Man, we live in the Garden State. That's what it says on our license plates, anyway," said Jon Bon Jovi, the lead singer. "We were pretty scared following somebody like Merle Haggard . . . ."

But we're getting ahead of the story here.

The town of 58,000 residents was busting at the seams with all sorts of music-loving folks a couple of days before scores of big, customized tour buses rolled in carrying the singers and their bands. Families slept in campers. Long-haired, full-bearded good ol' boys wore souvenir T-shirts from Hank Jr. concerts stretched tight across their beer bellies. Pink-haired punks came in black leather and studs. Blue-haired grandmas wore white polyester pants suits. Kids from the university dressed in the school colors of orange and blue.

Remember how Wavy Gravy woke up the sleeping masses at the original Woodstock by announcing "breakfast in bed for 400,000"? Well, at 6:00 on this Sunday morning, fans were filing by the tens of thousands into the University of Illinois football stadium. They were greeted by thousands more who had spent the night inside the stadium.

At daybreak, pretty young women were already perched on the broad shoulders of their boyfriends standing on plywood covering the Astroturf. Willie and Family were out singing "Whiskey River Take My Mind" while roosters were still crowing across the farm belt.

Oh, and it rained at Willie's Woodstock, too.

"Sure I could be home watching it on TV," said sleepy, soaked Kenny Fisher, a fortyish fellow from southern Illinois who wore a cap advertising Caterpillar earthmovers. The 18-hour-plus shendig, featuring 112 acts, was televised live on cable TV's Nashville Network as well as by a hodgepodge of local stations across the country.

"But this is something I can tell my grandchildren about someday," explained Fisher.

Indeed.

There were Billy Joel and Randy Newman pounding out "Stagger Lee" on their dueling pianos. The crowd roared when the Beach Boys sang the line about "Midwest farmers' daughters" in their classic "California Girls" song and actress Debra Winger jumped on the stage and danced to "Barbara Ann." A church choir is white robes sang back-up for the rock group Foreigner. Carole King played the piano and sang songs from her "Tapestry" album. Joni Mitchell recalled growing up on a Canadian wheat farm.

Sissy Spacek, daughter of a county agent in rural Texas, served as hostess and introduced performers Glen Campbell, Loretta Lynn, John Denver, Alabama, Kenny Rogers, Don Henley, Charlie Pride, Lou Reed, B. B. King, Arlo Guthrie, Joe Ely, John Fogerty, Neil Young, the Nitty Gritty Dirt Band, and, by God, George Jones, the Possum hisself.

"I feel like going around and getting autographs," said Tanya Tucker as she wandered backstage wearing a floppy gray hat. It was rumored that Ricky Nelson was there just to watch.

"The energy is really good," admitted Carole King.

"This is a people-to-people thing. It has nothing to do with politics," said Charlie Daniels. "And if the American people don't grab ahold of it now, it won't have done no good."

Of course, even at $17.50 a ticket for the 80,000 or so who filled the stadium and much of the field and the millions of dollars more pledged on the phone lines, Farm Aid could hardly make a dent in the $200 billion in collective debt owed by America's farmers.

"There's a joke that the farmers tell around here that shows how things really are," said Tom Bicki, a professor at the University of Illinois' acclaimed School of Agriculture. "An Illinois farmer won a million dollars in a lottery and all the news people were asking him what he would do with all the money. He said, 'Well, it'll let me go on farming one more year'."

"Willie can sing and pluck all night long," says Don Murphy, who had to auction off his 240-acre farm in Henry, Illinois.

"But he's not going to make much headway with farm debt. We're in too deep," Murphy told Time Magazine.

Enrollment from the state's farm counties is down at the University.

"A lot of farm families can't afford to send their kids to school now," said Professor Bicki. "And a lot of the ones who can are telling them not to study agriculture. They see their family farm at a dead end."

And this comes at a college where farming is as much of the culture as fraternities and football.

Right in the middle of campus is a cornfield. It's the nation's longest running agricultural experiment. The first crop was planted on this plot in 1876 and the yield has been measured on the corn grown there every year since. When the university decided to build a library next to the cornfield, they put it underground so it wouldn't cast a shadow and skew the research.

"The main point of Farm Aid," says Illinois Governor James Thompson, "is to bring the plight of the American farmer to the attention of the nation."

And John Cougar Mellencamp brought the situation home with the lyrics to his "Rain on the Scarecrow":

"Rain on the scarecrow/blood on the plow/This land fed a nation/This land made me proud/And son, I'm sorry they're just memories for you now."

Nelson came up with some new lyrics, too:

"When you're farming for a living/And you make your money from the ground/Then you take it to the banker/But there ain't enough to go around."

"God bless y'all for coming," Kristofferson told the rain-soaked legions of fans after the heavens opened on a Sunday afternoon. "And God bless Willie for having us."

Amen, roared the multitudes.

Ol' Cooter

Followed by his hesitant family from Ward, Ark., (population 700), Kevin Bernard approached the former Georgia congressman perched on the hood of the orange '69 Dodge Charger and inquired, "You're the real thing, aren't you?"

Yessiree. It's ol' Cooter, all right.

Seven years after leaving Capitol Hill, Ben Jones is living his role as the greasy, good-natured mechanic on the "Dukes of Hazzard" and cashing in on the show's revival on cable by The Nashville Network.

From Thursdays through Sundays, Jones presides at a garage converted to the "Hazzard General Store" beside a two-lane highway winding toward the Shenandoah National Park.

"This ain't Disneyland," Jones cheerfully admits. "If we're open, I'm here. This is what it is—me talking to folks, posing by the General Lee, signing pictures, singing."

The General Lee, for those who never visited TV's Hazzard County, is the souped-up car with a Confederate flag painted on top that cousins Bo and Luke Duke took airborne every episode in eluding the greedy Boss Hogg and the bumbling Sheriff Rosco P. Coltrane.

The Charger parked beneath the "Cooter's" sign outside of Sperryville is one of 229 General Lee's used in the series, said Jones. About 1,500 vehicles of all sorts were wrecked during the seven years that the program ran on CBS, ending in 1985. Cooter spent considerable screen time driving a tow truck to pick up police cars that had smashed up chasing the Duke boys.

Few of the fans crowding around the orange car in Sperryville remembered Jones' brief political career.

A Democrat, he represented Atlanta suburbs from 1989 to 1993 before losing a primary, and his attempted comeback against Republican Newt Gingrich failed.

But the visitors all recognized the grinning fellow in the sleeveless shirt as "Cooter."

"I just happened to be passing by and saw the General Lee parked there," marveled Delbert Fioles, from Ponca City, Oklahoma. He promptly bought a $10 "Cooter's Garage" cap for Jones to autograph.

"I grew up with the 'Dukes of Hazzard.' I've still got the little Hot Wheels cars," said Chris Dodson of Chesapeake, Virginia. He drove his family an hour out of their way after overhearing a conversation about "Cooter's" at a McDonald's.

"It was my favorite show," said Vince Barrick, who lives nearby and brought his collection of character cards for Jones to sign. "I had all the matchbox cars and a scrapbook. It's good to have one of them living around here."

Cooter's souvenir store and museum of "Dukes of Hazzard" memorabilia opened on July 4, about a year after Jones and his wife, Alma Viator, moved into a log home in nearby Harris Hollow.

Viator runs a public relations agency in Washington, D.C., and met Jones when he was serving in Congress.

Since his defeat, Jones has resumed acting—appearing in the movie "Primary Colors" and a "Dukes of Hazzard" TV reunion, among other roles. He moved to Rappahannock County, Virginia after several years in Los Angeles.

"I've found a wonderful home here," he allowed. "The best thing is that people judge you by the way you are—not by how much money you have but by the way you behave."

Viator said the roadside "Cooter's" store "was a crazy idea that he had that I let go in one ear and out the other for a long time."

But in 1996, TNN began showing reruns of the "Dukes of Hazzard" twice a day and people started recognizing "Cooter" in shopping malls and asking for his autograph.

"I started thinking that maybe it wasn't so crazy," said Viator. "When we came here, nobody cared that he had been in Congress but they were excited that 'Cooter' was moving into the neighborhood."

Jones is happy to autograph "Cooter's" wares ranging from $4.50 pictures of the cast to $7.50 baby bibs to $15 T-shirts with cut-out sleeves like the ones he wears. Visitors can also buy local foodstuffs like "Daisy's Country Honey" and "Miss Alma's Apple Butter." Not for sale is an array of artifacts from the program—scripts, action figures, model cars, props, Cooter's costumes, off-screen snapshots of the cast, and even The New York Times obituary of Sorrell Booke, the actor who played Boss Hogg.

TNN has "introduced the show to a whole new generation of fans," said Jones.

Indeed, "Dukes of Hazzard" Web sites abound on the Internet.

Jones compares the show to the B-Westerns of old where action was paramount and the good guys always won. Children can watch the program with their parents, he said. "It's not cynical. Nobody ever gets hurt. I hear it every day from visitors, 'Thank you for putting on a show that was so much fun'."

Politics of Music Row

In Tootsie's Orchid Lounge—the smoky, historic honky-tonk hangout of singers from Patsy Cline to Kris Kristofferson—some stalwarts of modern country music were opining about presidential politics on a hot summer afternoon in 2004.

"Somehow country music got stereotyped as being right-wing conservative. But in reality, if you look at our executives, our artists, our audience, it splits down the middle like the country does," said Tim DuBois, a veteran Nashville music executive.

His own political skills were confirmed in convincing two stubborn, struggling solo artists—Ronnie Dunn and Kix Brooks—to unite as "Brooks & Dunn" and become the most celebrated duo since the Everly Brothers.

DuBois was not ideologically lonesome in the back room of Tootsie's.

"Speaking just for myself, I'm very, very much against the [Iraq] war," declared Bobby Braddock, a member of the Songwriters Hall of Fame whose decades of hits stretch from Tammy Wynette's "D-I-V-O-R-C-E" and George Jones' "He Stopped Loving Her Today," both co-written with Curly Putman, to Toby Keith's rap chart-topper "I Wanna Talk About Me."

DuBois and Braddock are among the leaders of Music Row Democrats.

Now, the conventional wisdom is that Democrats are about as plentiful in Nashville's recording studios as Republicans are on the movie sets of Hollywood.

When the Music Row Democrats held their first meeting in late 2003, "I went because I wanted to see who else was going to show up," joked John Scott Sherrill, a songwriter whose hits include "How Long Gone?" by Brooks and Dunn, "Modern Day Drifter" by Dierks Bentley, "Church on Cumberland Road" by Shenandoah and Josh Turner's song, "Would You Go With Me?"

But, lo and behold, by 2006, there were enough twanging, downhome Democrats to form an impromptu group dubbed the Honky Tonkers for Truth who put out a CD cut entitled "I'm Takin' My Country Back

But the singers said the song didn't get any airplay on country music radio stations—mainly because of lyrics like these:

"And I'm takin' my country back/Boys you ain't been doin' her right/Oh, I've been watching you and I don't like/How you been treating my Stars and Stripes. You took our jobs and sent 'em overseas/Now we owe billions to the Red Chinese/You blew the budget and you botched Iraq/So I'm taking my country back."

The song is one of twenty on a CD released online by the Music Row Democrats to remarkably faint fanfare.

"Conservative Christian Right-Wing Republican Straight White American Male" is another cut on the CD by Todd Snider, an artist who arrived in Nashville after stops in Austin and Atlanta. Or, as Snider describes himself "a tree-huggin,' peace-lovin,' pot-smokin,' porn-watchin,' lazyass hippie."

While conceding that country music is widely perceived as a bastion of conservative politics, the Democratic group claims a membership of about 1,200 in "the industry," including a slew of guitar-picking liberals.

However, many have kept their political views to themselves, cautious after the Dixie Chicks saw their records struck from radio station playlists and were forced to cancel concerts because of slack ticket sales after their well-publicized criticism of President Bush.

"They took a real palpable economic hit" for voicing their views at a concert in England, said Sherrill

Of course, there is no shortage of Republicans on Nashville's famed Music Row, home of the country music industry.

One is Bob McDill, another Hall of Fame songwriter whose string of hits range from Alan Jackson's "Gone Country" to Waylon Jennings' "Amanda."

"The Democrats always play the same ole tune—'We're going to punish those fat cats'," said McDill. "But the money doesn't go to the poor. Five out of six tax dollars go to the middle class in what is a transfer of wealth in exchange for votes."

"The majority of country music listeners in Tennessee and across the country are Republicans and conservatives," said Chris Devaney, executive director of the Republican Party of Tennessee. "The message being delivered by the Music Row Democrats is not one that would resonate with these types of voters."

Tootsie's Orchid Lounge, where pickers and singers perform live country music from 10:00 a.m. until 2:00 a.m. daily, is located across an alley from the Ryman Auditorium, the original home of the Grand Ole Opry.

In the decades before Opryland, performers would leave the stage at the Ryman—the "Mother Church of Country Music"—and sneak out a stage door to Tootsie's for a beer between sets. Singers from Faron Young to Willie Nelson frequented Tootsie's and the walls are covered with hundreds of pictures of past performers who played there before hitting the big time.

The country music fans in such blue-collar bars should be Democrats—not Republicans, said Bob Titley, executive vice president of TBA Enterprises, an entertainment management company, and a founder of Music Row Democrats.

These working class people often vote against their own economic interests in supporting GOP candidates, he lamented. That's because Republicans have diverted their attention from jobs and wages to "social issues" such as gun control or abortion, Titley claimed.

"Gun rack, ball cap/Don't take no crap," Trace Adkins sings in his hit, "Rough and Ready."

"I'm a Second Amendment Democrat," Titley said, indicating his support for the right to bear arms. "But how often does a gun law affect me? It never affects me."

But the perceptions of the politics of Nashville and Hollywood have led to rumors of intimidation.

In Hollywood, some actors believe movie roles could be lost if their Republican loyalties were known, said Sherry Jeffe, senior scholar at USC's School of Policy, Planning and Development. And, citing the example of the Dixie Chicks, some country music singers believe Democratic leanings could cost them radio play.

"In Los Angeles, conservative voices feel more stifled and in Nashville liberal voices feel more stifled," said Titley.

Some singers have joined the Music Row Democrats. Emmylou Harris, Hal Ketchum, Pam Tillis, Rodney Crowell, Allison Moorer and Raul Malo of the Mavericks have performed at Democratic "Kerry-oke" fund-raisers.

"But they're not currently on the radio much either," noted Braddock.

Unlike Hollywood's movie stars, mainstream country music stars usually keep their politics to themselves.

"I don't feel the need to talk about politics," Martina McBride told the Nashville Tennessean. "Maybe it's a Midwestern thing, but I was raised where your political party is kind of private. It's nobody's business."

"Why would you take a stand when you know that taking that stand might alienate about half of your audience?" asked DuBois. "Because you're not in this for politics. You're in it to entertain people."

"Particularly in the mainstream portions of their careers," country music stars "know they would cleave their audience in half" by pushing one presidential candidate or another, said Titley. "So most tend to be reserved."

And there is a reluctance to rile up radio stations.

"I don't think there's a political agenda [with stations or chains] that goes down as far as punishing an artist on a particular release because of his politics," said DuBois.

But Titley—who said he doesn't think his politics had anything to do with him no longer managing Republicans Kix Brooks and Ronnie Dunn—said the hard-working folks who listen to country music are ripe for the Democratic message.

He said this message is delivered in lyrics on the CD, which could be downloaded for $20 from the group's website at www.musicrowdemocrats.com

"Now I'm stocking shirts in the Wal-Mart store/Just like the ones we made before/Except this one came from Singapore/I guess we can't make it here anymore," James McMurtry sings on his cut, "Can't Make It Here Anymore."

"Katrina came. Katrina went/The money we need had all been spent/New Orleans or Baghdad, it's all the same/And the contracts are written in Halliburton's name," sang Tim O'Brien in his cut, "Republican Blues."

Over hamburgers at Brown's Diner, a Music Row hangout, Sherrill and Orrall said it would be pointless to pitch such songs to record executives. While pro-war songs like Darryl Worley's "Have You Forgotten (About Bin Laden)?" and Toby Keith's "Courtesy of the Red, White and Blue" are played on country music stations, audiences hear few, if any, lyrics that are anti-war.

In their mission statement, the Country Music Democrats say their founders "were fed up with feeling as if they had to apologize for being Democrats."

And they insist their industry is more politically diverse than widely believed. Even Toby Keith has described himself as a "lifelong Democrat" and Tim McGraw said he may one day run for governor of Tennessee as a Democrat.

On the other hand, Chely Wright's song, "Bumper of My SUV," received considerable radio play. It is about a getting an obscene gesture from "a lady in a mini-van" who doesn't like the singer's bright red bumper sticker saying United States Marines.

"And yes, I do have questions/I get to ask them because I'm free," Wright sings. *"That's why I've got a sticker for the U.S. Marines/On the bumper of my SUV."*

Like many country music songs, Robert Ellis Orrell's contribution to the CD was inspired by a true-life incident—when he discovered that Al Gore had become his Nashville neighbor after the 2000 presidential election. In the song, he marvels that despite winning the popular vote, "Al Gore lives on my street."

The former vice president even makes a cameo on the cut.

"Hey Man, I like your song. But you need to get over all that stuff," Gore says. *"Hey, this is a great neighborhood."*

Storytellers Convention

Settle back for a spell. There's a yarn to be spun. It's about liars and listeners and a graveyard with ghosts in a tiny mountain town where the truth has been lost.

Y'all see, they held the annual National Storytellers Convention here not long ago.

The talkers came from all over to Jonesboro, a village stuck high in the Great Smokies near the place where Tennessee, North Carolina and Virginia all come together. They told tales; spread gossip, legends and legacies; sang ballads; swapped stories. Facts were rare but hyperbole was rampant.

There was the lament, for instance, of the daddy whose only son was so ugly that the boy had to ambush breakfast. That boy was so ugly that the doctor who delivered him took one look and then slapped the baby's mama. And the child was so mean and destructive that if you gave him a banana to play with, he would use it to tear up a ball bearing.

The storytellers recalled cold winters. One old fellow remembered back to when his shadow would freeze to the ground and he would have to chip it off his feet before he could walk on. That same winter the flames in the fireplace froze solid and had to be ground up into red pepper.

At the convention, such stories started Friday and didn't let up until sundown Sunday.

Saturday dawned bright and cold. The brick sidewalks downtown were filled early with visitors. There were young men and women in down-filled vests and faded jeans, older women in long flannel dresses with bandanas covering their hair, men in black turtleneck sweaters and tight black britches; folks who looked rural and dressed in plaid shirts and bib overalls. Most everyone had a scrap of calico pinned to a pocket—the badge showing admission had been paid to listen to the stories.

The townspeople of Jonesboro were also out. The ladies of the Westside Church of Christ had a sidewalk cake sale going. A loaf of nut bread went for $3.50. Across Main Street, the Rainbow girls had a competitive table laden with cakes and cookies. Lavender's Supermarket had red mountain apples, orange acorn squash and multi-colored ears of Indian corn displayed outside. Inside, sales of hot coffee and homemade vegetable soup kept the old-fashioned cash register ringing.

When the clock chimed ten o'clock atop Washington County's white-columned courthouse, the tales took up where they had left off the previous evening.

There were three big tents where featured storytellers displayed their talents. In one, a blond woman from New Hampshire named Mara Capy used dance and chants to tell an African folk story. She was followed by Gamble Rogers, a lanky, craggy-faced fellow from Florida.

In the green-striped tent, with the air fresh with the scent of recently cut grass, Gamble Rogers offered observations: "An expert is just an ordinary man away from home. A rich redneck is one with a rusting Lear Jet up on blocks in his front yard."

He recalled bits of graffiti: "The Moral Majority is neither."

Then Gamble Rogers, who calls himself a Twentieth Century troubadour, launched into a rift about Still Bill, an alleged citizen of Habersham County, Georgia. It seems that Still Bill contracted conjunctivitis in both eyes, requiring him to cover both with black patches. Instead of staying in and listening to TV, though, Still Bill set out on a walk. He was guided by his three-legged dog, Flat Tire. Casually eating an almond joy, Still Bill maneuvered past the gas station, pool hall and Unitarian Church—that's the one with a lightning rod on the steeple.

Just then, a Doberman Pincher pushed past Flat Tire and used Still Bill's leg for a fire hydrant. When the temporarily blind man with a wet leg started feeding his Almond Joy to the offending canine, it was too much for an onlooker.

"Bill, that Doberman just irrigated your foot," he said. "Why in the world would you give him your candy?"

"Fool," Still Bill replied. "I'm just trying to figure out which end to kick."

After Gamble Rogers left the tent, in came Ray Hicks, an herb farmer who lives on Beech Mountain, so far in the North Carolina backwoods that it took a festival organizer three hours to drive to his house to pick him up. Ray Hicks doesn't drive himself since he wrecked his truck on one of the winding mountain roads.

Ray Hicks tells traditional Jack Tales—"Jack and the Beanstalk" being only the best known of this seemingly endless series. Hicks told one where Jack, the hero, encounters Hardy Hardhead and his mules, This Way and That Way.

The oration was as spirited outside the tents as inside. Under the hickory and sycamore trees, a swapping ground was established where anyone could get up and tell a story and anyone could try to top it. As the sun burnt away the morning chill, stacked bales of hay became bleachers as listeners came and went while the stories never stopped.

Chuck Larson, a big bellied man from Georgia with a blond goatee going gray, told some of the best tales. As a boy, he recalled, he had trained a bass fish to be his pet. The bass learned to breathe air, walk on his fins and sleep in a box behind the wood stove. He was house-broken. Why the bass would even go fishing with ol' Chuck. But, sadly, on one of these outings, the fish fell into the pond and drowned.

"It is a fact," Larson swore. "Why, I would eat fried chicken before I would tell a lie."

$$\sim$$

The festival got started in Joneboro—so the story goes—after Mayor Jimmy Neil Smith heard comedian Jerry Clower on the radio and decided to bring him here to tell his homespun Mississippi stories. That was in 1972. Since then, a truly national convention of storytellers has evolved.

"It's a gathering place for people throughout the country, sort of a reunion," said Mel Burton, a storytelling librarian for children who brought his own brood here from St. Louis. "There are a lot of well-known storytellers here—not just the ones who are featured either. They're all over the place."

The growth of the festival has been both reassuring and alarming to Connie Regan and other organizers from the National Association for the Preservation of Storytelling. The popularity proves the enduring value of the arts of oral history and entertaining. But storytelling is founded in a fragile connection between talker and listener. Crowds and TV cameras can cheapen the experience.

"I really believe the festival is for the immediate experience between storytellers and listeners," said Regan. "It's not that we don't want the media here. But we don't want them to interfere with that experience."

Filming, taping and still photography are discouraged in the tents. Reporters are tolerated, not wooed.

It's a contradiction to have TV cameras recording the festival because organizers want to win people back to the oral tradition and away from their TV screens.

~

There was a supper time break Saturday, then more stories through dusk. As darkness settled, folks just naturally meandered up the street to a grassy spot beside Jonesboro's historic cemetery.

Near the grave of Caroline Dosser, wife of James, who died in 1854 at the age of thirty-nine, blankets were spread. It was time for the telling of ghost stories. Boys found perches on tree limbs. Children snuggled against their parents, seeking warmth against the night air and security against the scary tales.

A huge bonfire was lit.

David Bolt, a Carolina banjo picker, began the stories. He told about the fiddling ghost of Rattlesnake Ridge, a place not far from this very graveyard.

Sure enough, as he worked the magic of words, the sound of fiddling drifted in on the night wind.

~

PASSIONS

~

Dogs of Glory   *Photo by Rick McKay*

Endless Love: The Legends of Bitsy Grant Tennis Courts

Bifocals make it harder to smash overheads. Headed down from the apex of a lob, the fuzzy tennis ball seems to leap as it passes the boundary between near and far sightedness on the split-level eyeglasses of the elderly.

But the aged champions of Bitsy Grant Tennis Center have adjusted to failing eyesight, as they adjusted when they lost a step, then two and no longer had the speed and sinew to race to the net and recover to the baseline.

"You have to adjust your game. You get old. You lose your quickness. You play in the middle of the court so they can't drop-shot you," said Dr. Glenn Dudley, a seventy-two-year-old retired physician who has played at the public tennis center since it opened about three decades ago.

"I've played here every day since I retired," recalled Dr. Dudley, who is known as "Foots" because of his medical specialty. "But then, I played here every day before I retired, too."

As steady as the sun, the old-timers come to the courts that are set amid a rolling meadow and shade trees on the north side of Atlanta. Dr. Dudley is but one of a group of white-haired regulars from the center who have won an astonishing array of national and regional seniors championships.

Any two of them can most likely beat you and your doubles partner out of $10 in a quick set.

Bitsy Grant himself, the winner of forty-four national tennis titles and still a graceful player at seventy-two, serves and volleys most afternoons on the courts that bear his name. Bobby Dodd, the seventy-four-year-old former Georgia Tech football coach whose name graces the college's gridiron stadium not far away, limps gamely on bad knees along the baseline and strains to reach the corner shots with an over-sized racket.

Larry Shipley, Tom Bird, Nat Collins, Hank Crawford—these players and others have stocked the clubhouse with trophies for decades.

"I remember these guys when they were in their forties. They've gotten more competitive as they've gotten older," said Ralph Foster. "I came here in 1954 and the same guys are playing on the same courts as they are now. Then and now, they all want Court One."

Sometimes they call him Tennis Center Ralph, because of the way he answers the clubhouse phone, "Tennis Center, Ralph."

The nickname is apt. Foster and the center have long been linked.

"It's in my blood," he conceded. "I've been here over half my life."

A friendly, black-haired craftsman of the tools and condition of a tennis court, Foster has studied the collision of racket strings and hollow ball millions of times. He assesses serves and strokes with a knowing eye, although he never took up the game himself.

"I just never had the time," he explains.

But Foster understands this hallowed place where the graceful, albeit not always genteel, game of tennis has long been played with skill and zest.

"Bitsy Grant is probably the only place in the world where you could see the president of a bank and its janitor playing together. They're all just tennis players here," said Foster, describing this downhome mecca of athletic meritocracy. "It's a home for most of them, especially the old seniors."

Foster knows the rites of the center. Position is earned. When a new player shows up, the manager said, the veterans "are almost like bulls."

A newcomer must prove himself, playing the worst of the regulars first, working his way up until he finds his competitive level.

"There are a great bunch of seniors," said Nat Collins, a relative youngster at 68. "That's what keeps Bitsy Grant going. It's known all over the country for its seniors."

"Everybody is getting older now, so winning might not be as important as it used to be," he continued. "But I don't know. It's still pretty important."

Victories are long savored.

Hank Crawford recalls an afternoon fifteen or more years ago when he sat with some of the other seniors in the clubhouse to plan a trip to the national championships in Knoxville, Tennessee.

"When it got to pairing up, they left me out," Crawford recalled. "I said 'That's okay,' and called up this old boy I knew in Kansas City to be my doubles partner."

Crawford and his Kansas City partner won the tournament, beating two Bitsy Grant regulars in the final match. It was only one of about fourteen national championships that Crawford has won, but it is the one he still chuckles over most. And, of course, it is the one that comes up most often in his conversation on the veranda at Bitsy Grant.

The courts have been open to the public since the center was completed in the early 1950s. The cost of playing is cheap. Court fees are $2 per hour per player and yearly memberships are about $200.

Price is not what made the Bitsy Grant center exclusive. Quality tennis is.

"Nobody cares if you've got a dime or a million dollars out here," explained a longtime player. "As long as you can hit the ball between the lines."

"You can always find somebody who can whip you, and that's what makes it challenging," said Crawford. "I belong to a country club but I hardly ever go there. I go to Bitsy Grant because of the competition."

"Good tennis. Good camaraderie. We don't want nothing changed," said Max Klenberg, a seniors player who is also a member at a tennis club in Palm Beach, Florida. "There's better weather in Palm Beach, but there's a better grade of tennis here."

Hugh Manning is another colorful piece of the Bitsy Grant mosaic.

The club pro drives to the center every day in an immaculate, cherry red, 1965 Corvair, its trunk full of tennis rackets and pastel balls.

Manning has taught tennis lessons at Bitsy Grant for fifteen years and has played here for more than twenty. He is a trim, tan, talkative man.

What he talks about is tennis.

Manning says Bobby Riggs once trained at the Atlanta center. If he had worked out there before his ballyhooed TV match with Billy Jean King, Riggs would have won, Manning maintains.

It was right here on a side court that he taught Hank Aaron, the major league home run leader and Hall of Famer, how to play good tennis, Manning recalls. The former Atlanta Brave outfielder was just patting at the ball.

"I told him to grab the racket with two hands like a baseball bat and swing it like one. Then I bounced him a ball. He hit it about a mile."

In a matter of minutes, Manning said, he showed the home run king how to groove his natural baseball swing to hit a tennis ball. Now Aaron is a good tennis player, he said.

"Atlanta is a good tennis town," the old pro said. "There are thousands of tennis players here."

And most of them would benefit from one of his lessons, observed Manning, who instructs compulsively whenever he sees anyone hit a tennis ball. Watching the seniors play at Bitsy Grant, Manning issues a constant critique and barrage of advice.

Mostly it is ignored. Another ritual.

Inside the clubhouse, the competition continues at card tables. There the games are gin rummy, checkers or bridge. Every five years or so, a Ping-Pong table is put up and the small ball is paddled to and fro for a month or two. No matter what the game, there is always a buck or ten riding on the outcome.

There are separate seasons for parlor games. "They do those games like sports," said Foster. "Summer is checkers season. They play bridge in the fall. Winter, it's gin."

Winning is as important inside as it is on the outdoor courts. Gamesmanship is rampant.

The wrinkled, bowlegged old codgers who sandbagged you out of a sawbuck on the tennis courts are equally adept at lightening your wallet at the card table.

"Oh, we have a lot of fun, and, you know, fellowship," deadpanned Crawford. "Checkers. A little gin rummy. Just for fun."

"There are some pretty good checkers players," poor-mouthed Collins. "Just like there are some pretty good tennis players."

Inside and out, wagers are made not so much for the money as to intensify the thrill of victory and the agony of defeat. Paying up prolongs the loser's agony and pushes him harder to win the next time.

On the veranda of the clubhouse, a Spartan setting with bare tables and hard chairs and no carpets, the regulars sit and talk and watch the tennis. There is a reverence for the seniors but also a brutal assessment of their game.

"Coach's game has slipped in the past year," observed one graying player, watching Dodd play doubles partnered with his son, Bobby Dodd, Jr., who is called "Brother" around the center.

"Coach plays tougher with Brother than with anyone else though," the observer added.

Crawford, a champion at every level since his collegiate days, now uses a weighted racket as a compensation for the passing decades.

"With that thing, the harder you hit the ball at him, the harder it comes back at you," laughed Manning. "So to beat him, you have to dink little shots just over the net and make him run and carry it."

Death, of course, reduces the roster of players at Bitsy Grant from time to time.

Red Enloe, a Bitsy Grant entry, was struck by a heart attack and fell dead on the court at a tournament in Fort Myers, Florida, where many of the center's other seniors were also competing.

"He had six brothers who died of heart attacks before they were fifty-five," said Crawford. "He made it to seventy-three. He told me one time that he was living on borrowed time, that everybody in his family had heart attacks young. He was a good old boy, one of our regulars."

They come to the courts rain or shine, hot or cold.

"I have to open for half a day on Christmas," said Foster. "I closed one year and somebody broke the lock."

Their grandkids give them sweatsuits and rackets for presents and they want to break them in.

"They've played 'til the lines couldn't be seen under the snow," said Foster. "At zero degrees they came out. I saw eight seniors playing with socks on their hands."

All-Night Gospel Sing

The Bible had urged them to make a joyful noise unto the Lord. And, Lord knows, they responded.

From mid-afternoon Saturday to just before dawn Sunday, the tenors hit the sweet, high notes and the basses hit the rumbling, low ones for a Christian audience that clapped in time and appreciation.

For the twenty-seventh consecutive year, the all-night gospel sing had come to this town of tobacco warehouses and railroad yards that sits on the edge of the Okefenokee Swamp in southeastern Georgia.

"We're going to give you that good, old-time, hand-clapping, foot-tapping type of song," the first singers promised.

"Hallelujah!" the faithful responded. It was time to lift voices in praise and thanksgiving.

They had come from all over the South, more than 20,000 strong, to a high school football stadium for a sing advertised to last from sundown to sunup. They spent the afternoon arranging lawn chairs and coolers in front of the stage on the football field and listening to amateur groups harmonize.

Hovie Lister, a veteran gospel musician, explained how this affair was born nearly three decades earlier. He was with the Statesman Quartet back then, playing in courthouses and churches across Georgia. Lister and Doc Browning, a druggist and Shriner, hit upon the idea of a gospel sing to raise money for a hospital for crippled children.

"I always thought it would go. I knew the people of South Georgia love gospel music," explained Lister. "It was critical, though, that we decide on the best time for it. All the farmers sell their tobacco in August, but they're usually through by the end of the month. So we decided it would always be the last Saturday night in August."

They would go all night, he said, "because we wanted to give people all the singing they wanted to hear."

Now it has grown into one of the biggest events in gospel music.

"You can go into any city in the United States and say 'Waycross' and there will be somebody who has been to it," said Doc Browning. "Say 'Waycross' and they'll say 'that's where the sundown to sunup sing is.'"

The fans came in legions on Saturday. Clean-cut, blow-dried Sunday School kids wearing creased jeans and T-shirts that praised Jesus. White-haired women who came prepared with cardboard fans to stir the hot air and to shoo the gnats. Barbered men in open-collared, short-sleeved shirts. Pretty young mothers with frosted hair. Blue-eyed babies sucking pacifiers. Farmers in John Deere caps and starched bib overalls.

They filled the old grandstand, facing the grass, goalposts and fence that still carried advertising from when the Waycross Braves played here in the Class D Georgia-Florida League. The ones who came early and well provisioned set up picnics and chairs on the ground. They ate fried chicken, slabs of cake and boiled peanuts, washing it all down with soft drinks.

Outside the stadium, rows of recreational vehicles were filled with families. Yolanda Chaney and her daddy had driven over from Valdosta on Friday to get a prime parking spot. They watched the Ware County High School Gators play a high school football game in the stadium the night before the sing.

Saturday afternoon, a multitude of family and friends joined Yolanda and Lin Chaney, a ritual for thirteen straight sings.

Gospel music fans have greater loyalty than followers of country or rock music, allowed Lister, who had formed a quintet called the Masters Five that is made up of members of other famous groups. Along with Lister, it includes James Blackwood of the Blackwood Brothers, Jake Hess of the Imperials, J. D. Sumner of the Stamps Quartet and Rosie Rozelle of the Statesmen.

A kinship forms between gospel groups and their fans, Lister said. "They form sort of a family for us."

"These people are all church people, all religious people," said James Blackwood. "Most of these people wouldn't go to a rock concert—ninety-five percent of them wouldn't be caught dead at one. Twenty-five percent might go to a country concert. But they're mainly gospel fans."

Gospel music goes beyond entertainment to "spiritual blessings," said Lister. "You'll hear amens out there.

"These are extremely patriotic people. Mostly average, middle-class in income. But you'll find doctors and lawyers, too. People who were raised in the country. People who went to little country churches and have heard some of these songs all their lives. They bring back memories."

Onstage, Lister speaks to the crowd in with the cadence and fervor of a hard-shell Baptist preacher. Gospel fans are faithful, he and Blackwood agree, but they expect a certain code of behavior. God will forgive sinners, but gospel fans won't buy their records.

At about 8:00 P.M., the Saturday night singing gets going in earnest. Clasping hands, the crowd stands and joins together in "Amazing Grace."

"It's the Christian national anthem," says an on-stage singer. The familiar words of the old hymn ring out, ". . . I once was lost, but now I'm found, was blind but now I see . . . "

"You've got a lot of people here that this is about the only type entertainment they're allowed," said Leroy Powell, a cameraman for an Atlanta TV crew that was taping a documentary of the sing. He looked toward a group of women without make-up, their hair in buns, and wearing dresses to their ankles. They don't drink, dance, take drugs or run around, he reckoned. "Joyful noise is about all they've got."

But the message from the stage was not one of hellfire and damnation.

"You don't have to go around with a long face to have religion," said a Kingsman. "If you think that, you ain't got religion. You've got indigestion."

Don Stallings and Tom Bowman were among a group of families who had come from Albany, Georgia, and Jacksonville, Florida, for a picnic, fellowship and the music.

"I probably like country music as good as gospel," said Stallings, who owns a collection agency in Jacksonville. "There's not that much difference in the beat and all. But I like people who come to gospel sings better."

"I go to church. I'm a Christian. This kind of crowd is more like me. A country crowd is a little rougher," said Bowman, a tool dealer in Jacksonville.

Onstage, the Masters Five come out in black tuxedoes and ruffled shirts. They end their act, as do other groups, with a pitch for record sales.

"I know that all of you here tonight, if you have a record player, you'll want to this album," says Blackwood.

Indeed, after their stints on stage, all the singers become salesmen—hawking records, pictures, scrapbooks and bumper stickers in the bowels of the old stadium. Down where the Shriners sold popcorn and Cokes and the women's clubs of Waycross had cakes for sale, gospel groups set up merchandising centers. Sales were brisk.

A gospel record might not quickly sell as many copies as a country hit, but it will continue to sell at a steady pace for longer, said Blackwood.

"God bless you. We love you," the Hinson Family tells the fans. "Let's go buy some records."

The Hinsons were singing when the rains came.

On the grass, fans put down their Instamatics and opened umbrellas. In the stands, there was a scurrying for shelter. But the music continued, inspiring some in the audience to stand and shout for joy and raise their palms in the air to catch the Holy Spirit. Soon the rain stopped.

The seven major groups all finished one set and some went on to seconds in the dark hours before dawn. An old man snoozed in a lawn chair. Boys in jeans and jerseys played touch football out behind the stage. Musicians caught cat naps in the big, customized buses that take them from show to show.

Gradually, the crowd began to thin. By sunup, most everyone was gone. They left humming hymns and hoping for a few winks after breakfast.

Then it would be time to go to church.

Friday Night Religion

Ralph Smith has closed the Jesup Pharmacy early, an action that he takes only on autumn Friday nights.

"A lady called awhile back and asked if it's true that I close for football games and stay open during church time," recalled the friendly pharmacist. "I imagine that she thought it was terrible, but I told her, 'yes ma'am. It's true'."

After all, they hold church two or three times every Sunday and on Wednesday nights hereabouts. But the Wayne County High School Yellow Jackets play football games only ten times a year—unless they make the play-offs, of course.

"If they tee the ball up on Friday night, I'm going to be there," declares Smith, a former mayor of this southeast Georgia community. "Frankly, I can't understand anyone who doesn't want to go."

He does, however, understand Kenny Bryant—who once drove from his military post in Fort Walton Beach, Florida, a distance of several hundred miles, to see one quarter of a Yellow Jackets football game.

Bryant, now a CPA and president of the local Touchdown Club, played guard for the Jackets during his high school days. He pauses to ponder when a visitor asks him how important high school football is to Jesup.

"Well," he finally opines, "it's not as important as God."

But it might rank second.

In Jesup—as in many small Southern towns surrounded by piney woods—high school football is regarded with a reverence and ritual that comes close to being spiritual.

"Football—to us—is a religion," admits Smith.

And the whole town stands solidly behind the coach and the boys on the field—win or win.

"If winning wasn't important," said one Jesup fan, "God wouldn't have made scoreboards."

~

The September sun is setting over the woods behind the stadium and five serious, respected men—wearing bright gold trousers—can only wait now to see whether their charges are prepared to prevail this week.

A town waits, too, as teenaged boys—like their fathers, brothers and uncles before them—cover their shoulder pads with jerseys of gold, white and black, the colors of their school. Most of these players have striven for these fleeting fall evenings for most of their lives. In Jesup, daddies put tiny footballs in the cribs of their infant sons and boys buckle on helmets in the youth leagues before they can read. Now, for most of the seniors in the cramped locker room, this season will end what has been the biggest part of their young lives.

This is the 11th autumn of playing organized football in pads for Ronnie Teston, a sixteen-year-old senior who goes both ways for the Jackets—playing offensive center and defensive end.

"I started when I was five," said Teston, a blond boy with a cleft chin. He knows this will likely be his last season, that he is too small to play college football.

"I wish I had one more year. I hate to even think about not playing," said Teston, whose older, bigger brother plays for the University of South Carolina. "You can tell yourself you're glad it's over, but I really won't be. I've played for so long now. I really love football."

Teston and his teammates are waiting to play Tompkins High School from Savannah. Although they have already won twice and lost once this season, this will be the Jackets first sub-region game. The seniors don't need coaches in gold britches to tell them that winning would help extend their experiences into the play-offs.

As the team kneels in prayer in the locker room, a warning drifts over from the stands: "A Jacket sting is a powerful thing."

Like the players, the teenaged girls wearing a big "W" on their chests have longed for these Friday nights.

"I always wanted to be a cheerleader," says Melissa Horton, a pretty, freckled fifteen-year-old junior who started cheering in youth leagues when she was in grammar school. "It gives you status in school. Everyone looks up to you."

Also like the players, the cheerleaders earned their Friday night glory through competition. A panel of teachers and former cheerleaders judged their individual routines in rigorous tryouts. Only winners prance on the sidelines—whipping a goodly portion of the populace of Jesup into a pregame frenzy.

"It feels great," admits Lauruby Lathan, seventeen, a senior cheerleader. "You wouldn't believe how great it feels."

~

Jesup, with 10,000 residents, may have gotten its name because it is the seat of Wayne County. In the smaller neighboring communities like Gardi and Odum, this was the main town located "jes up" the road a piece. Or, perhaps, it was named for General M. S. Jesup, an Indian fighter of some renown.

U.S. Highway 341 serves as Jesup's main street. There are more churches in town than bars. The ITT Rayonier pulp mill is the major employer. Pine trees are cultivated in surrounding woodlands.

Jesup is also where Len Hauss, who went on to become an all-pro center with the Washington Redskins, first fastened a chinstrap. This is where Bear Bryant recruited the great end, Raymond Ogden, to the University of Alabama. Ogden was a farm boy who, legend had it, plowed without aid of mule or tractor. The list of Jackets-made-good goes on and on—to include Lindsay Scott, the flanker whose touchdown reception against the University of Florida helped win a national championship for the University of Georgia.

"I believe no other town of this size in the United States has produced as many college football players," allows John Donaldson, coach of the high school team and a former Jacket himself in the 1940s who went on to play with distinction at the University of Georgia.

"This little town never backed off from playing anybody," said Jim Sullivan, the white-haired owner of S&R Men's Shop. "It gets ahold of everyone. Every time a TV announcer said 'Len Hauss from Jesup, Georgia,' it made the whole town proud."

~

The countdown to kick-off for the Tompkins game begins at the bonfire Thursday night. The mountain of planks, logs and cardboard has been lit prematurely. Just who the culprits were remained a subject for conjecture by school officials the following day. The flames shoot up with the band, clad in jeans and Izods, still practicing its formations. Wearing white shorts and gold V-neck tops—one of their nine separate outfits—the cheerleaders mount a flatbed trailer and begin the yelling.

In the soft edges of the firelight, young parents sit with their toddlers. On an adjoining street, boys in cowboy hats drive candy-colored pick-ups equipped with chrome roll bars and oversized tires. A local boy, his arm in a sling, is visiting from college. He recently had surgery for a football injury suffered two seasons ago.

"I wish I was still out there playing," he says longingly.

Atop the trailer bed, the girls lead the town in singing the high school alma mater. "Cling to the things that are right and Wayne County High."

Most everyone joins in.

~

Football is the glue that bonds Jesup's generations. Jim Buie's boy, Ty, is the Jackets' second-string quarterback this season. The elder Buie, production manager at the local paper, which comes out twice a week, was the quarterback himself in the late 1950s and early 1960s.

"Back then, football set you apart. To have that football jacket set you above the crowd," remembers this son of a sawmill worker. "You'd go downtown, people would know you, talk about the team. To a lot of us ol' pore boys, that meant something."

Buie doubts that playing football means as much to his son and the rest of the current crop of Jackets. But he may be wrong.

Victor Drawdy, an articulate senior who toils with skill in the anonymity of the offensive line, understands the gravity of football.

"Since I started kindergarten, it was all I ever heard about. My parents got me started in football before I was six years old. I ain't ever known anything else," he said. "Everybody always said how big I was for my age and how I ought to play football.

"When you're little and playing midgets and all, it's fun to play. But it's different now. It's like a job or an occupation."

Did Drawdy, seventeen, ever consider quitting?

"Well," he admits with a grin, "a few times out there on the field in camp, it did run through my mind."

Football camp—two weeks of torture immediately before the start of school—is a rite of manhood here. Players leave their homes, cars, mamas and girlfriends behind for seemingly continuous practice at some secluded spot.

Nowadays, "camp" is held on the lawn of the Rayonier plant and players spend their nights at the Jaycees fairgrounds. But for two decades, Jesup's boys went to Parker's Paradise—a hunting camp deep in a swamp, seven miles from the nearest neighbor and even further from the comforts of civilization.

"The highlight of the day was pumping well water to drink at the end of practice," said Dink NeSmith, publisher of the Wayne County Press-Sentinel and a guard on the 1966 Jackets. "Basic training in the army was a letdown after going through football camp."

A milk truck would make daily run to camp, but the driver was unsympathetic to pleas from boys seeking a ride home. Still, attempts to escape are legendary. One player hiked to the river, caught a ride on a passing boat to the highway, then hitchhiked to town. Another was spotted trudging down a dusty back road, his electric fan in hand.

"When they got home, their daddies would bring them right back," said NeSmith.

This seemingly harsh act was actually one of fatherly kindness. For in the eyes of his peers, men he would know likely throughout life, such a boy would be forever branded a weakling who quit camp.

Does Dink NeSmith, a successful businessman who thinks football helped him in life, want his sons to play?

"I'm not going to take a stick and stand over them and make them," he said with a smile. "But yes. . ."

~

Tricia Bennett Armstrong would like for her daughter to be a cheerleader.

Perky at thirty-two, the blonde working mom runs a photography business with her husband. She was a cheerleader her junior and senior years of high school. Then, as now, the last period of the school day was devoted to the craft—practicing routines and yells and making signs promoting school spirit.

"When I think back about high school, the first thing I think about is cheerleading," she said. "When I go to the games, I look at the cheerleaders and think that's the way I looked . . . Lord, the outfits are cuter now, though."

Her daughter, Amy, was the mascot cheerleader a couple of years ago and still wears her outfit to elementary school on Fridays, said Mrs. Armstrong.

She hopes her daughter will share what she had: "Standing in front of the crowd . . . Leading cheers . . . Seeing all those people get excited."

Likewise, Kristin Phillips wants her daughters to know the fulfillment of being a majorette.

"It seems I always had a baton in my hand from the time I was five on up," said Mrs. Phillips, now a newspaper employee in her early 30s. "I remember before I even started school I'd watch band practice. I always assumed I would be a majorette from then on."

Since majorettes had to be part of the band, she learned to play the clarinet in order to be eligible to twirl. She was solo twirler her junior and senior years and earned all-state honors. Her daughters, aged five and two, both have batons, now.

"The older girl shows an interest," said mom.

Pat Jones, a senior linebacker, figures that he knows why some boys become football players and some don't.

"A lot of it is your parents," he said. "If they start you off right."

~

Under the Friday night lights, Sammy McCray, the Jackets senior full-back, is ready to kick off to Tompkins.

Earlier, he had explained how he doesn't worry on pre-game afternoons. "When I get taped, that's when I start getting my mind on the game. By the time I hit the field, I'm ready to play. I can't be thinking about nothing but football then."

Now, at 8:00 P.M., that's the common thought of people all over Wayne County. Up in the press box, Charlie Hubbard has begun the play-by-play report over radio station WLOP. "Everybody who's not at the game is listening," explains the announcer, whose daughter, Jean Anne, was a cheerleader a few seasons back. If the broadcast is interrupted by technical problems, the station is immediately beset by phone calls from complaining listeners.

Thompkins, wearing blue-on-blue uniforms, receives the kick-off but soon punts. The Jackets drive to Tompkins twenty-five yard line. From there, tailback Vince Clark sweeps right end and scores. The kick fails and WCH leads 6-0.

Later that first quarter, Clark throws a tailback pass to split end LeRoy Robinson, who pulls it from a defender and scores. The play covers sixty-five yards but is called back when an official declares offensive interference. The crowd moans and boos.

Tompkins drives and scores the next quarter. Their extra point kick is blocked. The score is 6-6 when the half ends.

As the band stands ready on one end of the field, Coach John Donaldson leads his team off the other.

~

"When I heard Donaldson had been hired, I said 'Jesus has come back to save us'," joked Jim Buie, who holds the down marker on the sidelines to get a closer view of Jackets games.

Donaldson, a star running back here and later at the University of Georgia, first became head coach in Jesup in 1952. His teams won the AA state championship in 1954 and 1959 and the sub-region championship every year until he left. He went to the University of Florida as an assistant coach and later to a similar position at the University of Georgia. Clint Madray, another Jesup native, coached the Jackets for the twelve years that Donaldson was gone. He became the high school principal when Donaldson returned.

So for the three decades following 1952, there have been only two coaches—both local boys made good—at the high school. But in 1979, when Donaldson had his first losing season ever at 4-6, there were rumblings of discontent amongst the townfolk.

"A high school coach is accountable to the general public," acknowledges Donaldson. He recalls receiving two new cars from the community following good years and was prepared to withstand the heat of a lean season.

"I've seen both sides now."

He has not been afraid to confront controversy. Although the stadium was built by Jaycees, the coach took exception when some members of the civic group brought flasks of whiskey to warm up during Jackets games.

"They don't drink in church, do they?" asked Donaldson.

And they don't drink in the stadium any more either.

"It's not easy for a hometown boy to come back," said the coach. "But I've never brought disrespect on Jesup in my life."

Over the years, he has coached some great players. "But I've got more respect for the boy who doesn't get to play much than for the stars," he said. "The boy who practices faithfully and then sits on the bench has learned a lesson. And most times, that boy will make it in life.

"He's got to be a good person. It's hard dealing with the criticism, answering the question, 'Why don't you get to play?' It's hard to admit you're not good enough. You've got to have some solid things behind you."

~

The third quarter ends with the score still 6-6. In the final period, Thompkins—an oddessey from a first down—runs an improbable draw play and miraculously keeps the drive going. They score, make a two-point conversion, and lead 14-6.

With time running out, the Jackets try another tailback pass. It flutters up like a startled quail and is batted by a receiver and then a defender—right into the hands of halfback Stan Carter. He runs unmolested into the end zone. Clark then runs in for the two-point conversion and the score is tied 14-14.

The cheerleaders' hair-dos are melting in the humidity when the clock runs out. "What happens now?" one asks. The game goes into overtime, delaying the start of the student council dance at the gym.

When two five-minute overtime periods end with no further scoring, Tompkins is declared the winner, 15-14, on a complicated penetration ruling. They moved the ball closer to the WCHS goal more often. A dejected team and town leave the stadium silently.

~

On Sunday morning, with church bells pealing down the road, the fellows sitting at the Jesup Pharmacy soda fountain are still discussing the game. It's a real soda fountain—serving up handmade milkshakes and cherry Cokes—but the men are expected to pour their own coffee.

"We just got whipped," says Ralph Smith.

Others blame the loss on the Jackets touchdown that was called back by the referees—"worse decision I ever saw."

"That same referee cost us a game over in Waycross two years ago," recalls a regular. "I thought he got disbarred after that."

But the group is good-natured despite the defeat.

There are six more Friday nights to look forward to this fall.

Farming

They met at the wedding of his brother and her friend from nursing school. A year later, they said "I do" to each other.

It was a good match—rooted in shared values that their forebears had cultivated over generations of tilling the Southern soil.

She grew up on a North Carolina tobacco farm in an era when neighbors helped each other pick the broad green leaves and hang them in weathered wooden barns for curing. His ancestors had raised cattle and corn on the hilly western edge of the Shenandoah Valley for over a century.

From the start, they loved each other and they loved the land and they loved the lifestyle. They lived near his folks on the farm that his daddy had purchased in 1929. Although hard work and hard times were never strangers, satisfaction was their constant companion as they raised a daughter and a son along with the crops and livestock.

Now, after more than three decades together, Wayne and Betty Cupp reckon that it is nearly time to retire and let their twenty-eight-year-old son, Maurice, take over this rural enterprise begun by his grandfather.

If only it would have rained sooner. . .

Although late August brought some relief, the drought in the mid-Atlantic states has been the worst since the Dust Bowl days of the Great Depression over sixty years ago. Stunted cornstalks withered in the fields.

Farmers were forced to ship cattle to market early because they couldn't afford feed. Pastures were sunburnt brown and crunchy. For most of the summer, about the only greenery was the paint on John Deere tractors sitting idle in sheds.

It was so dry hereabouts that University of Virginia scientists stuck radio transmitters on the backs of turtles and tracked one that trudged two miles—at an inch per step—to find water.

Worry is as bountiful as crops are sparse.

"My dad drilled the well in 1954 and we've always had plenty of water until this year. For the first time ever, the well water turned muddy," said Wayne Cupp. "We moved the cows to a pasture where the creek runs. Then the creek went dry. Then the pond went dry."

Luckily, the well revived and provided the several thousand gallons of clear water needed every day by the extended Cupp family and their cows, pigs and turkeys. Additional water from mountain springs was hauled in to save the backyard garden and orchard that provide vegetables and fruit to be canned or frozen for winter meals.

The garden "is not doing too well," allowed Betty Cupp. "Last year, I put up 100 jars of green beans. This year, I've done seven."

However, even with a wife and two children below the age of two to support, Maurice Cupp expresses no qualms about starting a career of fretting on the farm.

"Oh, we'll get through it," he says of the current troubles. "We always have."

But why would a family put out such effort generation after generation?

~

Despite the parched fields along the Eastern seaboard, enough rain has fallen across the heartland to produce bumper crops nationally and keep commodity prices depressingly low for farmers. Wayne Cupp estimates his break-even point on raising hogs is about 35¢ per pound, and last year he had to sell some for 15¢ a pound. So if he fattened a hog up to 400 pounds, he lost $80 at market for his efforts.

Increasingly, agriculture is being ruled by the economies of scale. The century's trend is toward fewer and bigger farms. Already, 80 percent of the nation's food is grown on 20 percent of the farms. Agribusinesses have swallowed up small family farms like Wal-Marts have squeezed out small-town merchants.

The Cupps own 108 acres in a scenic region coveted by developers. A neighboring farm recently sold for $6,000 an acre. Samuel Cupp, who died in 1991 at the age of ninety-six, paid about $100 an acre for the land now cultivated by his son and grandson. It doesn't take a calculator to figure that there's a huge profit in selling out.

But life is more than a ledger. The Cupps figure much of their sowing and reaping cannot be measured by what's in the bank, silo and deep freezer.

"I don't particularly like the economics of farming," said Betty Cupp. "But I like living out in the country. I like having room for a garden. I like the scenery. I like living in a way where kids learn responsibility by doing chores as they grow up."

For most of their marriage, Betty has worked fulltime as a registered nurse in the maternity ward at Rockingham Memorial Hospital in Harrisonburg, about twenty miles away from their farm.

"We depend on her salary at times like this," said Wayne. "I don't know what we would do without it."

"There are a lot of stresses," said Betty. "But when the kids were little, Wayne could make his own schedule to take care of them. If they were sick, he could take them to the doctor. We never had to hire a baby-sitter."

"My dad was here to help take care of them, too," recalled Wayne.

Their daughter, Laura, studied music education at James Madison University. Now thirty-one, she is married to a tax lawyer and lives in Sterling, Virginia, a suburb of Washington, D.C.

Maurice went to college for a little over a year, but his parents knew that his heart was always on the land.

"Farming kind of gets in your blood. When my son was growing up, I could see that in him," said Wayne. "But I let him make up his own mind."

"I would have discouraged him, but he doesn't listen," said Betty, with a smile.

"It's all I've ever known, all I've ever wanted to be," said Maurice. "There are probably some things I could do to make more money, but I guess you do what's in your blood.

"I like working for myself, being my own boss. I like the satisfaction of raising something up, whether it's crops or livestock. I appreciated the life growing up and I'd like to raise my children the same way. I want to teach them the value of work no matter if they go into farming or something else."

~

Wayne is sixty-four years old now, and Betty is seven years younger. Both had hoped to retire in another year or so, but the drought has put those plans on hold. It will take a while just to catch up. There won't be a corn crop this year, although the stalks will be harvested for silage to feed the cattle. Planted in swaths between cornfields, the pearl millet is usually cut twice each summer for hay. It is not tall enough this year for even one cutting. The cattle will likely just graze on it for a couple of weeks.

With no corn or hay for feed, the Cupps won't augment their herd by buying calves to fatten up over the winter and sell next year to feed lots. Indeed, they could have to sell off breeder cows to cut costs. But that would hinder a comeback when feed crops are better.

Still, there was plenty to do even in hot, dry times.

The elder Cupps rise at about 5:00 A.M. An hour later, Betty usually drives off to begin her 7:00 A.M. to 3:00 P.M. shift at the hospital, while Wayne takes the pickup truck to the turkey houses to check on the 20,000 or so young birds being raised under contract to the Rocco poultry company. There are two turkey houses on the Cupp farm—built at a cost of about $150,000 apiece—and Maurice has rented a third house on nearby property.

The poultry company supplies the birds and feed and medicines. The Cupps provide the houses, labor and water. The farmers' first check on the young turkeys is at 6:00 A.M., the last at 9:00 P.M. Alarms go off at any hour in case of problems such as a power outage. Disease can cull all profit from a flock and is a constant concern. In a good season, they'll make about $1 per hen or $2 on a tom, Wayne figures.

"Turkeys have a reputation for being dumb," Wayne says with a smile. "But I don't know which is dumber—the birds or the people dumb enough to raise them."

On her days off from the hospital, as summer ends, Betty cans and freezes vegetables and fruit from the garden. Blackberries are doing well despite the drought, and she prepared 100 jars of jelly and jam.

There are four kinds of tomatoes in the garden, along with sweet corn, collard greens, okra, beans, eggplant, cucumbers, peppers, onion, squash, rhubarb, and cantaloupes. Behind the blackberry bushes and grape vines are apple, peach and pear trees. The garden supplies about half the family's vegetables and fruit for the year.

Periodically, the Cupps will take a hog or cow to be slaughtered and butchered. The beef and pork comes back neatly packaged for the freezer. They get a good deal on poultry at the Rocco company store.

Y2K worries won't send the Cupps scrambling to the grocery store on New Year's Eve.

～

The pond that the Cupps stocked with bluegill, bass, catfish and minnows went bone dry. The adjoining hillside, normally a green pasture where cows graze, was transformed into a moonscape of exposed dirt and rocks. The long driveway was dusty between the white frame farmhouse and the turnoff at Waggy's Creek Road.

But there was always shade on the front porch of the house where Betty and Wayne reared their children and where they can now rock their grandchildren. They still feel serenity as they look out over the patchwork quilt of fields and pastures between their hilltop home and the Shenandoah Mountains. Every evening, the sun still sets in silence behind those mountains. Bo, the famously fast black dog once clocked at running 35 mph beside a car, still roams down Daniel Cupp Road—so named because it once led to the house of Wayne's great-grandfather. Maurice and his family live down that way now.

Whenever good times return to the Shenandoah Valley, the Cupps will be here farming.

Dogs of Glory

Her red hair ablaze against the azure autumn sky, Sam Furman waits in a Shenandoah Valley pasture with her anxious dog, Tucker.

At a judge's signal, she sends Tucker racing in a wide arc to settle silently behind four sheep grazing a quarter-mile away on the rolling field. Then, using a language of whistles, the handler directs her border collie as he maneuvers the stubborn sheep on a prescribed route over hills and across a dry creek bed, around a pole, through three gates and finally into a pen.

To keep the flock together, Tucker cuts right and left, starts and stops, glares and growls, sometimes lies motionless in the grass—but never touches the sheep—during an exhausting and agonizing journey. A digital clock counts down the thirteen minutes allowed for completion of the course.

Several hundred spectators sit behind a wire fence, having come from all across America to watch and run their own dogs in the twentieth annual National Sheepdog Finals Trial. A venerable sport in the British Isles, this obscure, exacting—and expensive—pastoral pastime is rapidly gaining popularity in the United States. In ten years, the number of dogs competing has tripled.

"I got a border collie," said Furman, an accountant from Suffolk, Virginia. "Then I bought a farm and sheep—the whole nine yards. My husband thinks I ought to be committed, but he's very nice about it. I had about $10,000 in expenses last year, and I don't do (trials) that much."

"It's addictive," explained Dee Lee, an insurance adjuster from Sanford, North Carolina. "You get a dog and a farm and some sheep and then bigger trucks, a bigger farm, more sheep, more dogs, a camper to take to trials."

And then, as often as not, the sheep at the trial won't behave meekly like, well, sheep. They'll baaa and butt and run off and flat-out refuse to be rounded up. Depressingly common are scores of "ret," when a handler "retires"—surrendering in frustration with dog and sheep still out on the course.

"This is the most humbling of sports," allowed Alasdair MacRae, a Scot who has become a legend among sheepdog handlers on both sides of the Atlantic. "If you draw bad sheep, it doesn't matter who you are or what you're running. It's the great leveler."

The newly shorn sheep at the National Finals Trial are Rambouilette wethers—castrated males—normally employed as ecological eaters. In the summers, they devour weeds beneath power lines in New Hampshire. In the winters, the herd moves to dine on kudzu along Florida roadways. In both cases, their appetites allow states to reduce the use of chemical herbicides.

Although the trial is open to all breeds, only border collies are competing. These bright, energetic and athletic dogs are bred to herd animals and have evolved into what competitors here say are the world's best sheepdogs. The 150 competitors have earned their spots through their performance in state and regional trials.

Tucker is an exception in that most of the competing dogs have monosyllabic names: Bob, Cap, Jim, Kate, Roy, Meg and so on.

"There are some two-syllable names, but better something short and sharp" for issuing quick commands, explained MacRae.

The handlers are as diverse as the dogs are similar. Some own cattle ranches or sheep farms or even poultry flocks and use border collies in their operations. A few are professional dog breeders and trainers. Most are hobbyists: doctors, lawyers, salespeople, housewives or others with a love for dogs and a passion for competition that compels them to spend weekends in motorized campers parked in pastures where trials are held.

"People just get the bug," said Bruce Fogt, who grew up raising sheep near Sidney, Ohio, and is publisher of the Working Border Collie magazine. "They buy a farm and some sheep and shift their whole life over for it."

About 70 percent of the sport's participants are hobbyists and the rest are ranchers or farmers, Fogt estimated. "Those percentages used to be reversed," he said.

While unfamiliar to most Americans, sheepdog trials have been a staple of the British Broadcasting Corporation for a quarter century. The BBC program "One Man and His Dog" takes viewers to trials in Scotland, Ireland, Wales and England.

The U.S. championship was held at Belle Grove Plantation, just outside Middletown, over a week in late September. Handlers from around the country came, sporting silver shepherd's whistles on rawhide necklaces and swapping dog stories.

"I'd always heard that a man gets only one good dog and one good wife in his life," opined a toothless fellow in a cap advertising a dog food. "But I've had several good dogs."

Nobody else has ever had a dog like Alasdair MacRae's Nan—dubbed "the Michael Jordan of border collies" by The Wall Street Journal. Nan is the only sheepdog ever to win the British International and the U.S. National Finals. She set the record score—108 out of a possible 110—on "One Man and His Dog." She's going for a "three-peat" at Belle Grove Plantation, having won the nationals in 1997 and 1998.

But Nan is nearly ten years old.

"This is probably her last finals," said MacRae. "She's getting stiff. She's just not as quick and athletic as she used to be."

A ruddy, friendly fellow who speaks with a rich brogue, MacRae is the son of a tenant farmer from the highlands of western Scotland. As a teenager, he went to work with a shepherd who also trained dogs. Young MacRae decided to turn sheepdogs into his life's work. It wasn't long before his dog Mirk won the Scottish championship. Nan is Mirk's granddaughter.

In the mid-1990s, MacRae came to the United States on his honeymoon and decided to stay. He lives on a farm near Shipman, Virginia, with his wife, Cindy, and their 6-month-old daughter Ceilidh. To make a living, he said, "I do a little bit of everything"—training and breeding dogs (a trained border collie sells for $1,500 to $10,000), conducting clinics for handlers, judging trials, winning prize money. The top prize for the National Trials is $1,000.

MacRae has a second dog, Cap, entered in the finals trial and is philosophical about the coming day when Nan can no longer compete.

"She's done what I wanted her to do for the last seven years," said MacRae. "Now it's time for her to do what she wants to do."

But what border collies want to do is work.

To discipline the dogs for mistakes, trainers simply don't work them for a couple of days, and "they get the message," said Mike Canaday, president of the Border Collies Handlers Association.

Border collies are working dogs, not show dogs, he said. In herding cattle or sheep, "a dog can do the work of three or four men."

Sheepdog trials are set up to test the skills that a dog and shepherd would use during a year of work, MacRae explained. But only about five percent of the border collies at the National Trials are regular farm dogs the rest of the year, he estimated.

The preliminaries last three days and cull the field from 150 dogs to fifty for the semifinals on a Saturday. Nan barely makes the cut. Then she is among the twenty dogs that make the Sunday finals. The border collies must deal with a flock of fifty sheep, and the tasks are more complex. For example, they have to separate several sheep with collars from the others.

Against all odds, Nan wins her third title.

"It was one of the best runs of my life!" exclaims MacRae. "Best not to count her out too soon."

Visit to a Small Town

Beneath a brutal sun, the rocking chairs and swings are empty on the broad, graceful porches of this small Southern town. Air-conditioning keeps the populace inside except for the short, sociable time after supper when the heavy heat of summer eases and gossip can commence without sweat.

Warrenton, the seat of Warren County in the east Georgia piedmont, has been hit hard by a recession. A big sawmill has shut down and nearly fifteen percent of the residents are out of work. Jobs are hard to come by in a county of 6,583 residents, only about a third of whom live within Warrenton proper.

The town surrounds the courthouse. Stores on Main Street close every Wednesday afternoon. Hard liquor sales are banned, but beer and wine are sold legally—except on Sundays, of course.

There are more black folks than white folks in Warrenton and they live in different neighborhoods, divided roughly by the railroad that runs through town. But residents on both sides of the tracks are much alike. The men—regardless of skin color—are likely to own guns, drive pickups, tend backyard gardens, hunt and fish, and talk about football. The women put up homegrown vegetables in the late summers and make sure their families are in church pews come Sunday. Everyone frets because the young people have to move away to find work.

~

"The boll weevil chased me away from Warrenton in 1923," recalled John Henry Howard, as he sat in front of an electric fan in his house trailer. One of ten children born in a tenant-farming family, he went north with thousands of other black Southerners when the cotton crops failed. He worked and lived in Detroit and New York until 1978. Then Howard and his wife, Addie, returned to their hometown.

"This is my ending-up place," Howard explained. Now, at seventy-seven, he plants and hoes in a backyard garden and rekindles friendships interrupted half a century ago. He has good health, can live comfortably on his savings and Social Security, and allows that his troubles are few.

"I've hated debt all my life," he said. "I like to know when I lie down, I can go to sleep without worrying about how I'm going to pay my bills."

He can't understand folks who buy so much on credit cards or those who can't find a job, even if it takes uprooting as he did so long ago.

"When I was coming up, my daddy taught me to give an honest day's work. To do justice for your paycheck," he said. "And I got along fine and I didn't have no trouble holding a job right up 'til I retired.

"The biggest problem now is that young people are not on the right road."

Addie Howard, sixty-four, agrees.

"They say, 'I won't do that kind of work.' I say you do anything until you can find better," she said. "You do anything to earn your way as long as it's honest."

John Henry and Addie Howard still work hard. Behind their trailer are rows of corn, peas, lima beans, string beans, pumpkins, turnip and mustard greens, okra, cucumbers and tomatoes. Mrs. Howard cans and freezes vegetables all summer to eat the following winter.

Warrenton seemed bigger when he left, said Howard. The town's race relations have changed "90 to 100 percent" since those segregationist years of Jim Crow laws restricting the rights of black residents.

"I registered to vote as soon as I got back," he said. "If I'm going to live in a place now, I'm going to participate as a citizen."

~

Allen Howell keeps a pistol in his right front pants pocket as he cuts the hair of the men of Warrenton.

"It's a high-standard Derringer. It shoots two bullets: .22-caliber, Magnum hollow points. The bullet goes in and then spreads out," Howell explained.

There are two barber shops on Main Street. Each has a single chair and one barber and each charges $4 for a haircut. Customers choose one place or the other, not so much on how their hair gets cut as how they regard the barber as a friend. Only a hardware store stands between the striped poles of the two shops.

The hardware store almost got held up a month or so ago, said Howell. The would-be robbers tried to make off with the store's fishing-license money. They dropped the loot as they were chased out by a clerk with a shotgun. The suspects probably would have escaped then, but their getaway car overheated on the highway to Thomson and the police caught them.

What's wrong with America today is that criminals are coddled, said Howell, and it doesn't do any good for a jury to sentence a murderer to die because some do-gooder appeals court judge will keep the killer alive anyway.

"I think they ought to put a scaffold on every courthouse square and hang them there until the buzzards eat them," said Howell. "You wouldn't have to do but one of two like that to stop some of these murders."

Not that there are all that many murders in Warrenton, of course. The barber shop is more threatened by the loss of trade that it had when Howell's father was cutting the hair of the scores of farmers who would come in to get a shower as well as a trim.

"I wouldn't see my daddy at all on Saturdays," he said, recalling the era when few farms had indoor plumbing. "He'd leave home before sunup and we'd fall asleep listening to the Grand Ole Opry on the radio before he got back."

Men still come in, often to just sit and talk. The sheriff gets a $2 shave every morning.

"It's a rest home," Howell laughs. "They come in to get away from their wives."

But the cash register rings less regularly.

"The trouble is that the young folks have to move away. There are no jobs to hold them in Warrenton," said the pistol-packing barber. "And more and more of the old customers are going on to that great barber shop in the sky."

~

"For thirty years, my two boys have come in every morning between eight and nine o'clock and spent thirty minutes to an hour drinking coffee and talking with me," said Ocie Wilhoit, as she put out the china on a table on the screened-in porch. Known to generations of Warrenton citizens as Miss Ocie, she'll be eighty-five next month and has been a widow for seventeen years. The sons who visit her each day are graying businessmen.

She lives alone now in the handsome house with white columns that sits behind the courthouse square. It is filled with antiques and memories.

"Everything in it is old, including me. But I like it," said Miss Ocie. "It's right uptown so I know what everyone is doing. I sleep well at night in it."

Her husband was Jud Wilhoit, a lawyer and state legislator. The only time she ever lived away from Warrenton was from 1932 to 1941 when he served in the administrations of Governors Richard Russell and Eugene Talmadge. They lived in Atlanta then.

"But we always knew we'd come back," said Miss Ocie.

Her sons run a gas business from an office next to her house. Her daughter lives in near-by Augusta. Her grandchildren and great-grandchildren come to visit her. She has season tickets to the Georgia Bulldogs football games and still drives to Athens on autumn Saturdays for tailgate picnics with friends.

Across her front yard, Miss Ocie has watched Warrenton for most of her life.

"I think it's grown better," she said. "And it's on the move. For a long time, we just had one grocery store. Just recently another one opened—a Gurley's grocery store. And we're going to get an IGA store. Goodness, I don't know if Warrenton can support three grocery stores."

The Knox Theater is only a block from her front door but Miss Ocie said she hasn't seen a film there since "The Sound of Music." She doesn't cotton much to modern movies nor to much of what's on TV nowadays.

"I watch the game shows and the educational channel, but most of the rest I can do without," she explained. "Soap operas move too slow."

~

Jimmy Hammock is the woodyard foreman at the Union Camp operation just outside of Warrenton. Long pine logs are trucked there, sawed down, then shipped by rail to the Union Camp mill near Savannah. There these pines—known as pulpwood—are made into brown paper bags.

Hammock knows times are tough. One of his own grown sons is out of work. But the pulpwood foreman figures some things are all right, too.

"We're still in a free country, aren't we? That's good enough. And we're not at war."

~

SOUTHERNERS

~

Hokies   *Photo by Rick McKay*

Hokies

The nightmare followed Neal Ballas from his dorm room bed. "You wake up in the morning and don't want to believe it happened. But it did," said the twenty-one-year-old senior, slim and stiff and sad in the sharply creased uniform of the Virginia Tech Corps of Cadets.

"It was real. It was here."

On a clear, sunny spring Tuesday, there were none of the touch football games or friendly frisbee tosses that usually enliven the grassy green drill field in the heart of this sprawling campus. In a spontaneous, silent show of spirit and unity, practically every mourning student wore a maroon and orange hoodie, jacket or T-shirt emblazoned with the name of their beloved university.

They spoke softly of the thirty-three schoolmates no longer amongst them. Tears streamed down the cheeks of Jon Hess as he tacked a Virginia Tech hat to a wooden "VT" leaning against a maple tree that served as a makeshift memorial to the students killed by one of their own, twenty-three-year-old senior Cho Seung-Hui, the previous day.

"I was thinking, 'I'm here today. They're not,'" said Hess, a twenty-one-year-old senior from Grundy, Virginia. "I feel a lot of anger toward the killer and sorrow and I feel lucky to be alive."

On the bill of the maroon cap, Hess wrote a Bible verse: "Romans 8:31. What shall we then say to these things? If God be for us, then who can be against us?"

The stillness was eerie, the grim students said. The quiet was almost as strange as all the police officers and camera crews who suddenly populated the carefully groomed grounds that had seemed so familiar and secure such a short time ago. They wondered aloud if it would ever seem the same as it had before that terrible Monday in April.

"It's still really hard to comprehend," said Emma May, eighteen, a freshman from Chapel Hill, North Carolina. "As soon as you go outside and nobody is there, it really hits you."

It's like a comforting bubble that surrounded and protected them has been burst, explained Natalie Funte, nineteen, a freshman from Chantilly, Virginia.

"The whole campus is like this safe little family," said Funte, who lives in East Ambler Johnston Hall, connected by a corridor to where two students were shot to death. "People would open the door to people without pass cards. I've done it."

"It's still kinda unreal," said Brandon Stiltner, a senior engineering student from Grundy. "It almost seems like you're in a movie. But then it hits you again. And even if you don't know the people who were killed, you feel like you've lost a friend."

At the base of the "VT," there were white and red candles—thirty-two white candles for the slain students. Cho shot himself to death after his deadly spree. The killer's family can light their own candle for him, a student said.

Messages were scrawled on the memorial.

"We were all affected. All of us riddled with the bullets that tore through this campus," wrote CN. "The taste of this tragedy will never leave our mouths."

They will remember it like their parents remember when President Kennedy was shot and Vietnam War-era Kent State students remember when National Guardsmen shot the protesters and a generation of University of Texas students remember the shooter in the clock tower.

"We will never forget this day," Adam Hoover wrote on the makeshift memorial. "Rest in Peace."

With classes canceled for the remainder of the week, rugged stone academic buildings stood nearly empty. Some students wore backpacks and lugged duffel bags to cars and then drove off to sanctuary elsewhere.

Yellow tape bearing the words "Crime Scene Do Not Cross" separated Norris Hall from the sidewalk and drill field. The classroom building had been the bloody scene of most of the deaths. On Tuesday, three female students from northern Virginia walked to the yellow tape and left bouquets of daisies and carnations. They hurried away in tears—watched over by state police with weary faces.

A group of sorority sisters wore black ribbons on their orange Virginia Tech hoodies. Brisk wind blew yellow crime scene tape into the limbs of an oak. Somebody stuck a sign to a tree that said "God Bless Virginia Tech." A sobbing student muttered "media spectacle" as she strode past camera crews to lay tulips at the makeshift memorial. "I don't want to be on TV," she told them.

Inside the War Memorial Chapel, rotating cadets stood at attention beside a wreath.

"You always hear about something like this but you never think it will happen near you," said Rebecca Lindstrom, nineteen, a freshman from Charleston, South Carolina. "It's heartbreaking."

Somebody named Gary Franks wrote a message on the memorial "VT."

"Hokies: Stay strong. Come Together. We will be okay."

They came together as the sun set.

Hauntingly, the word sprang from thousands of young voices and echoed across the darkening campus.

"Hokie!" "Hokie!" "Hokie!"

"We came here not to dwell but to heal," declared Adiel Khan, president of the Virginia Tech student government.

In tight groups of friends, clad in maroon and orange, they had assembled around dusk on a giant lawn called the drill field, where generations of Hokies have assembled for pep rallies and spring flings. This night, though, they carried candles to memorialize fellow students who had fallen the day before in senseless massacre.

There were hugs and tears and angry glares at TV crews.

"Fellow Hokies, this is Virginia Tech," exclaimed Sumleet Bagai, a leader of Hokies United, a university association.

"Literally, this is the most united I've ever seen Hokies," said Bagai. "We organized as a way for our community to come together in times of tragedy. We were founded after 9/11 and came together again after Katrina."

This time the tragedy had come home, to their scenic campus in the New River Valley. This time the world was watching them.

A bugler sounded Taps. Far across the drill field, another bugler answered back. The notes sounded and rebounded. Again and again. Echo Taps is a tradition at major events.

The speeches stopped. The candles flickered. The word rumbled through the night.

"Hokie!" "Hokie!" "Hokie!"

Downhome in Manhattan

They were watching a Braves game on TV when Bobby proposed to Camille in this tale of glitz and grits.

"Ask me again," she demanded.

So he got down on one knee and asked again.

Not long afterward, in December 1986, U.S. Supreme Court Justice Harry Blackmun helped marry them at Peachtree Presbyterian Church in Atlanta.

Bobby is more formally known as Robert McDuffie on marquees proclaiming his appearances as guest solo violinist with orchestras around the world. His friendship with Justice Blackmun, who died last year, began while arranging a series of concerts at the Supreme Court.

Along with Otis Redding, Little Richard, Trisha Yearwood and others, McDuffie is a member of the Georgia Music Hall of Fame, located in his hometown of Macon.

"I'm the only one in a bow tie," he says.

Camille, meanwhile, is president of Goldberg McDuffie Communications, a New York publicity firm that represents authors and publishers. The agency helped coach Monica Lewinsky for her TV interview with Barbara Walters and arranged the book tour for "Monica's Story." The firm's clients range from George Jones, the country music singer, to Susan Faludi, the best-selling chronicler of feminism.

In a media-manipulating, commercial-culture biz full of outsize egos and insatiable expectations, Camille McDuffie is famous for being sweet.

"She's gracious, charming and tough," says Anne Rivers Siddons, who wrote "Downtown," "Low Country" and other novels of the New South. "I consider her a friend. She was raised very much like I was . . . and we understand each other the way a couple of Southern women who love literature would."

Like Bobby, Camille is from Georgia. She grew up in Atlanta.

After the betrothal, Camille's daddy observed that "bringing a violinist into our family is like pouring perfume on a hog."

If that sounds a tad like something Charlie Croker might have said in Tom Wolfe's bestseller "A Man in Full," there is a literary connection. Like the fictional Croker, Camille's father, Mack Taylor, is an Atlanta real estate mogul who opines with a drawl.

Then there's the fact that Wolfe brought his wardrobe of white suits to Atlanta and stayed with his friends Mack and Mary Rose Taylor while researching this epic on the New South. The author thanks Camille's parents in the dedication for their "insights and hospitality."

"Camille grew up hunting quail from horseback," marvels Bobby.

The McDuffies live in an apartment on the Upper East Side with their children, Eliza Jane, nine, and Will, six. There are toys on a hardwood floor beneath a Steinway grand piano. A Peter Max creation hangs on the pale green wall. There are scores of autographed books and a closet containing an Atlanta Braves jacket given to Bobby by then-Governor Zell Miller. The forty-two-year-old violinist is a diehard Braves fan.

As with any dual-career couple, daily life is hectic. School buses pick up Eliza Jane and Will in the mornings and return them in the afternoon. A nanny-housekeeper-shopper handles many of the household duties. For twenty to thirty weeks a year, Bobby is away on tour.

But this week, the couple's extended family has congregated in Atlanta for Bobby's performance with the symphony. Camille flew down with the kids. The McDuffies came up from Macon. Despite their years in New York, Bobby and Camille insist they're still "Southern to the bone."

Bobby moved to New York at age sixteen to study at the Juilliard School. His mother, sort of a grand dame of classical music in Macon, decided early on that her son was talented. She turned him toward the violin at age three.

His childhood lessons came from Henrik Schwarzenberger, a Hungarian refugee who had moved to Macon. But he listened to the Allman Brothers as well as Mendelssohn and sang in a church choir with Mike Mills, who plays bass with R.E.M.

"I hated violin practice," McDuffie recalls. "But I loved applause."

His life changed at fourteen. That was the year his mama pulled him away from playing basketball to attend a recital by Itzhak Perlman. His course was set when he heard the music that day.

He plays poker with Itzhak Perlman now, and practices violin five hours a day when he's home. He performs with the New York Philharmonic and other orchestras from San Francisco to Moscow. His classical CDs sell on several continents. He financed a $4 million Guarnerius, a rare violin made in 1735, to use in his concerts.

It was at one of these concerts that Bobby met Camille. A mutual friend from Georgia arranged for her to attend. Camille had moved to New York after graduating from the University of North Carolina at Chapel Hill. After the concert, she invited the homestate violinist to dinner.

"I thought he was really cute," she remembers.

He was impressed by her "charm and assuredness." From that meeting on, he aimed to marry her or somebody just like her.

"We call her the Fred Astaire of book publishing," says Lynn Goldberg, Camille's partner and the chief executive officer and founder of Goldberg McDuffie Communications.

Camille choreographs deals with such style that "you don't notice how much work she's done until you see the results," Goldberg explains. "You have to be very, very smart to not huff and puff in what, for most people, would be a very stressful job. But I think Camille finds it fun."

Basically, the job is to draw attention to new books. The tools are legion. Reviews in influential newspapers and magazines. Author interviews on TV talk shows. A recommendation from Oprah. Radio raves from Don Imus and NPR's "Fresh Air." A national tour for the author, with appearances on local TV shows and stories in local publications. Long lines of readers at bookstore signings.

Some writers are reclusive and must be cajoled and rehearsed for media encounters. Swamped with dozens of new books every week, journalists must be wooed to interview yet another author.

Maintaining relationships with an assortment of reporters, TV producers and such across the country, book publicists match personalities and interests to garner coverage and boost sales. In doing so, they deal with authors and journalists who frequently share an inflated sense of self-importance.

It's a backstage calling. "People often ask, 'Just what is it you do with books again?'" says Camille, forty.

When she entered the business seventeen years ago, she recalls, an independent publicity agency would almost always be hired by a publisher who wanted to augment the in-house campaign. Now it's mostly authors who realize the value of publicity and hire the agency themselves.

The authors with whom Camille has worked include Stephen King, Maurice Sendak, Umberto Eco, Gail Godwin, William Trevor, Sally Quinn, Melissa Fay Greene, Susan Cheever, Henry Grunwald, Bill Bryson, Harold Bloom, Kitty Kelley, P. J. O'Rourke and Anne Roiphe.

The closest she'll come to dishing is to describe Maria Shriver as "demanding." She loved showing George Jones around New York, recalling that the carefully coiffed singer brought a hairdresser as well as his wife.

She is more forthcoming about her own failings.

Mitch Albom's agent is a friend, and several years ago sent galleys of "Tuesdays With Morrie" for Camille and Bobby to read. She deemed the sportswriter's book "cliche-ridden" and turned down the publicity project.

"Well, obviously I didn't get it," she says.

"Tuesdays With Morrie" was on The New York Times Bestseller List for more than three years.

Dictionary Lady

Y'all want to know why Southerners say y'all?

In Dixie, y'all is used instead of you to address two or more people because it preserves the distinction between singular and plural that English used to have with the words you and thou.

You could look that up individually or y'all could do it collectively. It's explained on page 2072 of the American Heritage Dictionary of the English Language.

Even in an age of anchorpersons and MTV, such regional dialects are flourishing, said Anne H. Soukhanov, executive editor of this volume that chronicles the language as it's actually used by Americans and of several other dictionaries.

"It's rather interesting that even though we do have this CNN effect and this seamless language, that you can still, in Texas, sit under the shade of a ramada, which is a trellised walkway, or that somebody might hornswoggle you in the Midwest, or that down South, people still use words like goober and corn dodger," said Soukhanov.

"There is still a sense of local place and local community in our speech."

This lexicographer's lair is a tall, graceful white house with a sweeping lawn and a view of the Peaks of Otter in the nearby Blue Ridge Mountains. She was born in this home and four generations of her family have lived here since the construction in 1865. It is in an upstairs room with colorful rugs covering hardwood floors and with sunlight streaming through the blinds that Soukhanov puts together dictionaries.

Of course, she has some help. On one project, for instance, the veteran wordsmith led a global staff of seventy-two editors and an advisory board of forty-one English professors at colleges in the United States, Canada, Great Britain and Australia. They communicated mostly by e-mail.

Soukhanov, a slender woman of fifty-eight who speaks with a soft Virginia drawl, has authored and edited an assortment of books about words. She was Executive Editor of the *Microsoft Encarta College Dictionary* (2001) General Editor for the *Encarta World English Dictionary* (1999) and executive editor of *The American Heritage Dictionary of the English Language, Third Edition* (1992). In 1997, she co-authored *Speaking Freely: A Guided Tour of American English from Plymouth Rock to Silicon Valley,* and in 1995, she authored *Word Watch: The Stories Behind the Words of Our Lives.* From 1986 until last year, she wrote the "Word Watch" column in the Atlantic Monthly.

She helped edit linguistic guides ranging from *The American Heritage Children's Dictionary* to *Wall Street Words.*

She is passionate about the language and dismayed by its increasing misuse.

"All you have to do is to listen to TV newscasts." she said. "When a major anchorperson says, 'it's time for Bernie and I to sign off,' you know we're in trouble."

From this old house, she sees a global English-speaking populace with an increasing need for new dictionaries as the language expands ever faster.

The new-word explosion "started with 'sputnik' in the 1950s, continued with 'AIDS' in the 1980s, and gained velocity in the 1990s with the language of the Net and the PC," she said. Examples include "desktop publishing," "chat room" and "e-mail."

Now pop culture, worldwide TV and film broadcasts, cell phones and the Internet "propel new words into the national and international cultures much faster than before when people relied on print publications as the primary purveyors of new words," she explained.

"It's harder to keep up with the language now than it used to be. Dictionaries are going to have to come out every six to eight years rather than every ten to keep up with the adult vocabulary."

Before returning to the house where she was born "in the pink bedroom," she had lived for twenty years in South Hadley, Mass., commuting to Boston to work for the dictionary publisher. Then her mother died and she and her husband returned to her family home in Virginia.

"We decided to move back South."

She decided to regionalize a reference book after receiving letters from readers.

An editor at the Arkansas Gazette "wanted to know why the word 'tump' was not entered in any dictionary." Tump, of course, means in Southern speech to knock something over.

"I tumped the Coca-Cola off the table," she said.

Then Colonel Malcolm Brennan, a professor of English at The Citadel, asked her why "bodacious" wasn't in the earlier American Heritage dictionary.

"I said, 'That does it'," she recalled, and added dialectologists to the dictionary staff.

"Bodacious," by the way, is a Southernism for gutsy. The word was popularized in the "Snuffy Smith" comic strip and is probably a blend of the words "bold" and "audacious," the dictionary explains.

"There are many, many Southern dialects," said Soukhanov. "We've divided the country up into sort of a linguistic atlas" with overlapping subdivisions of the North, South, East and West. There are coastal terms, for instance, used all down the Eastern seaboard from Maine to the Keys and then along the Gulf Coast to Brownsville, Texas.

Some generalizations can be made about Southern speech.

The region gives its own meanings to words. To Southerners, for example, "favor" means to resemble another in appearance. He favors his daddy. "Ugly" means rude. Don't be ugly to your sister.

The dialect was influenced by the forebears of the modern South.

Words such as "yam," "goober" and "okra" have African roots. The term "juke" —incorporated into jukebox, juke joint or juked out—can be traced through the Gullah spoken by some black residents on South Carolina and Georgia islands to an African word meaning "wicked."

"Grits" comes from the Middle English word "grutta" meaning "coarse meal."

Native Americans contributed "hominy" and "pone" to the Southern dialect. "Tabby," the oyster-shell-based building material of the coastal South, comes from the French "tabis" but can be traced back further to Baghdad, Iraq.

The Southernisms "possum," "coon," and "tater" all came from dropping syllables from standard words. And some dialect is descriptive: "dirt dauber" for the wasps that build nests of mud; "longneck" for a beer bottle with a long neck; "go cup" for the plastic cup used to take a drink or beer out of a bar.

"We've preserved a lot more of our dialect patterns down here because we aren't quite as urbanized as the Northeast grid," said Soukhanov. "I have to 'carry' my neighbor to church, for instance. That's a Southernism."

Soukhanov's hometown has gained renown in recent years as the site of the National D-Day Memorial. Bedford lost twenty-one of its sons on the beaches of Normandy on June 6, 1944, in the Allied invasion of France.

After growing up in the central Virginia community, Soukhanov attended Randolph-Macon Womens College and then graduated from George Washington University in Washington, D.C.

"Daddy said, 'For God's sake, when you go to college, study something where you can get a job'," she said. She majored in Russian.

After graduation, she married and moved to Springfield, Massachusetts, where she got a job at Merriam-Webster. She soon learned that she loved examining and exploring words.

"I got hooked," she said. "If you watch how the language changes, you can see where society is going."

Battle the Barber

There was a time when customers would hitch their horses to the post in front of Floyd's Barber Shop and come inside for a 20¢ shave.

It was 1893 when William Marion Floyd opened the tonsorial parlor on Newcastle Street, the major avenue of commerce in this slow-paced county seat. Floyd's was already a local landmark when the newly hired, nineteen-year-old Howard Eugene Battle brought his comb, scissors and razor to the shop in 1928.

H. E. Battle never left.

For more than six decades, menfolk hereabouts have hailed him simply as Battle—the best barber in Brunswick. He has watched his customers march off to three wars, seen them suffer in the Depression and prosper in the '50s, shaped their hair into pompadours and ducktails and shags and buzzes.

And, at age eighty, Battle is still barbering.

"I don't want that rocking chair to get me," he explains.

"He is certainly a fixture in our community," says Wright Parker, whose family firm has been selling real estate in Glynn County since 1926.

Indeed, Battle has been the barber for the boys of five generations of some coastal clans.

"He cut my father's hair and his daddy's hair and mine," says Parker, who admits that his lifelong barber now has to search for strands to cut on his head. "He cut my children's hair and my grandchildren's."

"I hit seventy in May," Parker says, "and Floyd's sure was the first place I ever got a haircut in Brunswick. It is the only barbershop where I ever got a haircut in Brunswick, Georgia."

The longevity of Floyd's Barber Shop is even more remarkable considering that for many of those decades, it was the only black-owned business in a segregated Southern downtown. Its founder and the subsequent barbers have all been African-Americans, although most of the customers have been white.

"We never did have any trouble [on the racial front]," Battle says.

Integration is only one of the historic changes he has witnessed from behind the big, black leather chair.

Newcastle Street was paved with brick when Battle arrived in town after learning his trade in Atlanta and Vidalia. Georgia Trolley tracks ran down the center of the street, but the trolley cars were no longer running.

"I walked to work," he says. "I didn't have a car back then."

The 1930s hit the town hard. "We managed to hang on during the Depression because we had an old line of customers who stuck with us," Battle recalls.

Economic recovery came with World War II and the shipyards that were hurriedly built in Brunswick. In the postwar boom, a pulp mill would bring good jobs and a bad smell to the growing town.

Two high schools were in the county then—Glynn Academy for the white kids and Risley High for the black kids. Both had good football teams and both sent young graduates to fight in the far-off Korean War.

As the '50s progressed, more families bought televisions to watch the shows stations were broadcasting from nearby Jacksonville, Florida, and Savannah. Teenagers cruised the Varsity and the Pig 'n' Whistle and Twin Oaks. Jimmy Reed, the rhythm-and-blues legend, came to Selden Park and sang "Big Boss Man." With little fanfare, the town's black kids and white kids began going to school together in 1963.

Then the carefree boys whose dads had brought them to Battle for crew cuts grew up and went to Vietnam. Battle reckons his toughest times came in that long-haired period of the late '60s and early '70s.

"The Beatles were sure bad for the barbering business."

However, time seems to have little meaning in Floyd's Barber Shop. It remains Floyd's even though the namesake founder died decades ago, and Battle has been the main attraction as long as anyone can remember.

Battle has been married for fifty-nine years. He and his wife, Cynthia, who is from Cordele, Georgia, have no children.

Next to the barbershop, Battle has poured most of his attention into his church.

"Our church is over 200 years old," he said. "I used to be on the board of trustees, but I've let some of the younger folks take over those duties."

At its peak, Floyd's was a ten-chair emporium.

The shop had several barbers in the 1950s, but it was Battle who could cut a flattop with the most precision. There was always a wait for him on Saturday mornings, but there were no complaints. Boys could eavesdrop on the grown-up conversation and browse through the stack of *Playboy* magazines without fear of discovery by their mothers. Traditionally, women enter Floyd's only for the ceremonial first haircut of their sons or grandsons.

In other times, older boys would be dropped off while their mothers headed to shop at Altman's or O'Quinn's or the Lollipop. Now most of the stores have deserted downtown for the malls.

Floyd's decor reinforces the aura of a bygone era. For years, boys could see the personal shaving mugs that their grandfathers had kept at Floyd's for daily action. Battle still sharpens his straight razor on the leather strap hanging beside the barber chair and still wraps a customer's face in hot towels before lathering him and attacking his whiskers.

"But there are only a few left who want a shave," he said. "Occasionally, I'll do one. A shave is $5 now. A haircut is $6."

When he started, the haircuts were 35¢, the shaves 20¢.

Customers still wait in the hard hickory chairs where their fathers and grandfathers once waited. A replica of the Venus de Milo still sits in the front window. A traveling salesman left the statue there sometime beyond memory, and it has been a part of Floyd's Barber Shop ever since. The Venus is as ingrained in the lore of the place as Battle's marble stand and the tingly "Osage rub" that he administers to the scalp at the conclusion of a haircut.

Through the years, Floyd's has been in several locations along Newcastle Street. For a time, it was in the basement of the historic Oglethorpe Hotel. The town tore down the hotel, though, not long after it was featured in the movie "The View From Pompeii's Head."

Now the venerable barbershop is across the street from the Georgia Opera House—the building that housed the Ritz Theater when Brunswick's citizenry could still go downtown to watch a movie.

To this day, Floyd's does not have a telephone. Battle does not want his customers disturbed.

He is the lone surviving barber. There was a time when the shop's shoeshine boy would learn the trade in odd hours and eventually earn a chair of his own in Floyd's lineup.

But Battle's old colleagues are dead now. His old-fashioned barbershop is almost a relic among today's "styling salons," he said.

Last summer, some of Battle's longtime customers and fellow businessmen surprised him with an eightieth birthday party. They gave him the funds for a trip to Washington, D.C., to visit his 100-year-old mother.

Vacations are nice, Battle declared, but he said he has no plans to retire. It's true that many of his customers have white hair now, but some of the younger, more stylish patrons are just discovering that Battle still cuts the best flattop in town.

The Onion Fields

Six children of Hermelinda Ballesteros stooped in the onion field. The sharp metal clippers used to cut the tops and roots off the bulbs loomed huge in the small hands of Nena, the daughter who is eight years old and dreams of growing up to be a nurse. But throughout the warm spring day, the little girl steadily cut and bagged bunches of the pungent onions, pinching her fingers only occasionally.

Nearby, Nena's sister, Monica, pretty at thirteen and just beginning to notice boys, crawled down the long row of onions that a plow had just uprooted from the rich black soil of Toombs County. She wants to be a secretary some day in an air-conditioned office. But this day, she knew she must cut onions in a dusty south Georgia field. And she would cut onions the next day. She came here from Florida, where she picked oranges. She will leave soon, probably going to North Carolina, where she will hoe tobacco or pick cucumbers and bell peppers.

Hermelinda Ballesteros, who said she is divorced and from Texas, is proud of her seven well-behaved children. Amy, the youngest at four, is in a Head Start program for children of migrant workers in nearby Lyons. The other offspring, who range up to fifteen years in age, get 75¢ for every fifty-pound bag that they fill with cut onions. It was too late in the term, the mother said, for the older ones to start school here.

"They're good children," she said. "They work hard and they get tired, but I think they enjoy it, too."

Increasingly, Spanish-speaking workers harvest Vidalia onions—among Georgia's best-known crops. Growers said there are not enough local people willing to do the labor for the going pay.

"You ask somebody on the streets of Vidalia to do this work, and they'll say 'Hell no, that's minimum wage.' They'd rather get welfare. But these people just seem happy to get the job," said Ronnie Smith, a salesman for New Brothers Onion Growers, a Vidalia firm that owns one of the many fields where Hispanic workers are harvesting.

Growers find migrant workers are well suited for the onion farms—where large numbers of laborers are needed for short stretches of time when the onions are planted, transplanted and harvested. Farm owners contract with crew leaders. Their crews are willing to do work with a smile that many Georgians will no longer do at all, said Fletcher Jones, the sales manager for New Brothers.

"They don't ask much out of life," he said. "They're geared for work."

It's not just Vidalia onions that they harvest, of course. They pick citrus in Florida, produce in the Carolinas, peaches in South Carolina.

"We do the harvesting so all the people in the offices can eat," declared Roman Cruz Florez, a crew leader. "We are the people who do the harvesting so that there are vegetables in the cans at the grocery store."

Farming communities have welcomed the newcomers—some of whom are legal "green-card" alien workers and many who are here illegally.

"Us Georgians are a clannish lot, I know. We're usually suspicious of people who look or act differently from us," said Dan Mitchell, an official with the U.S. Labor Department's Migrant and Seasonal Farmworkers Association.

"But it seems that migrants are accepted around here. Maybe we just respect people who work hard."

Farmers find it easier to deal with one crew leader than to worry about hiring their own temporary workers.

But the crew leaders are often the cause of complaints among the workers, said Martha Jackson, who also works for the federal association. The laborers accuse crew leaders of cheating them in accounting for production or pay or withholding too much money for rent.

"I refer them to Legal Services, where they could get free legal help," said Jackson. "But when it comes down to taking real action, they always back away."

That's because a migrant worker's livelihood depends on his crew leader.

The leader scouts out the upcoming jobs—contracting with growers so that there will always be another crop to pick when present fields are bare. If the farmers don't provide lodging, the crew leaders finds places for his workers to live. He lends them money for gas and food to get to the next job. The leader is paid by the grower, then hands out the money to the workers.

Roman Cruz Florez is such a crew leader.

"For the last 30 years, this has been my job," he said, resting in the shade of an oak behind the gray frame house he has rented in Vidalia. Several cars, some rusting and set up on blocks, were parked nearby. Children played in the dirt and giggled in Spanish.

"I don't go out looking for people," said Florez. "They come to me and ask me for work. Anybody who needs a job can get one. They might not be legal, but they got to work."

Picking onions is piecework. At 75¢ per fifty-pound bag, some members of the Florez crew make $50 to $60 a day. The more onions you harvest, the more you make.

"If you don't work so hard, you don't make so much," said Florez. "If you don't work, you don't make nothing."

And when there is nothing to pick, no one on the crew makes anything.

"You've got to move, but you've got a job," said the crew leader, describing the economics of migrant labor.

Some of his crew members are part of his extended family and live in the rented gray house with Florez. Others live in trailer parks. Hermelinda Ballesteros and her children stay in adjoining rooms in a motel in the nearby community of Santa Claus.

"We have to pay $80 a week," she said. Working in the fields all day, she has little time to cook so the family mostly eats take-out from fast food restaurants.

"With this many people to feed, we're not able to get ahead," she said. There are no child support payments or alimony from her former husband.

The living conditions are crowded and sometimes squalid by local standards.

"They don't complain about where they live," observed Jackson, the federal worker. "You put some of them in better housing and a lot of them will just tear it up. Some of them will keep it cleaned up and nice, but a lot of them will just tear it up."

~

The distinctive odor of onions hangs over the fields where men and women and children are all moving bent-backed down rows of unearthed bulbs. The local workers marvel at the speed at which the Mexicans cut off the roots and tops and stuff the onions into green bags to be loaded onto flatbed trucks.

The pickers from Toombs County express no resentment toward the efficient newcomers.

"If they work cheap, I have to work cheap, too," said Doris Fay Gaffney, a twenty-four-year-old woman from nearby Cedar Crossing who has cut onions every spring since she was thirteen. "But we used to get 50¢ a basket. Now it's 75¢."

The baskets are emptied into green bags that are left standing in the fields and later loaded onto trucks. The fifty-pound bags of onions will fetch about $30 at roadside stands.

After picking the onions, workers are paid 1.5¢ per bag for loading them on the trucks.

Noe Florez, the twenty-one-year-old son of the crew leader, has spent his life in such fields.

"Sure I went to school. I went to lots of schools," he recalled. "My father traveled around and they took me with them. We just can't stay in one place too long."

Jaime Cruz, nineteen, hoists a bag and shrugs at his sweat and strain.

"I been doing it since I was born," he said with a smile.

~

KATRINA

~

The Funches Girls of Post-Katrina New Orleans   *Photo by Rick McKay*

The Algiers Point Militia

The Algiers Point militia put away its weapons Friday as Army soldiers patrolled the historic neighborhood across the Mississippi River from the French Quarter.

But the band of neighbors who survived Hurricane Katrina and then fought off looters has not disarmed.

"Pit Bull Will Attack. We Are Here and Have Gun and Will Shoot," said the sign on Alexandra Boza's front porch. Actually, said the woman behind the sign, "I have two pistols."

"I'm a part of the militia," Boza said. "We were taking the law into our own hands, but I didn't kill anyone."

She did quietly open her front door and fire a warning shot one night when she heard a loud group of young men approaching her house.

About a week later, she said, she finally saw a New Orleans police officer on her street and told him she had guns.

"He told me, 'Honey, I don't blame you,'" she said.

The several dozen people who did not evacuate from Algiers Point said that for days after the storm, they did not see any police officers or soldiers but did see gangs of intruders.

So they set up what might be the ultimate neighborhood watch.

At night, the balcony of a beautifully restored Victorian house built in 1871 served as a lookout point.

"I had the right flank," Vinnie Pervel said. Sitting in a white rocking chair on the balcony, his neighbor, Gareth Stubbs, protected the left flank.

They were armed with an arsenal gathered from the neighborhood: a shotgun, pistols, a flare gun and a Vietnam-era AK-47.

They were backed up by Gregg Harris, who lives in the house with Pervel, and Pervel's seventy-four-year-old mother, Jennie, who lives across Pelican Street from her son and is known in Algiers Point as "Miss P."

Many nights, Miss P. had a .38-caliber pistol in one hand and rosary beads in the other.

"Mom was a trouper," Pervel said.

The threat was real.

On the day after Katrina blew through, Pervel was carjacked a couple of blocks from his house. A past president of the Algiers Point Association homeowners group, Pervel was going to houses that had been evacuated and turning off the gas to prevent fires.

A guy with a mallet "hit me in the back of the head," Pervel said. "He said, 'We want your keys.' I said, 'Here, take them.'"

Inside the white Ford van were a portable generator, tools and other hurricane supplies.

A hurt and frustrated Pervel threw pliers at the van as it drove off and broke a back window.

Another afternoon, a gunfight broke out on the streets as armed neighbors and armed intruders exchanged fire.

"About twenty-five rounds were fired," Harris said.

Blood was later found on the street from a wounded intruder.

Not far away, Oakwood Center mall was seriously damaged in a fire caused by vandals.

"We were really afraid of fires. These old houses are so close together that if one was set afire, the whole street would all go up," Harris said. "We lived in terror for a week."

Their house is filled with antique furniture, and there's a well-kept garden and patio in back.

"We've been restoring this house for twenty years," Harris said.

There are gas lamps on the columned porch that stayed on during the storm and its aftermath. The militia rigged car headlights and a car battery on porches of nearby houses. Then they put empty cans beneath trees that had fallen across both ends of the block.

When someone approached in the darkness, "you could hear the cans rattle."

"Then we would hit the switch at the battery and light up the street," Pervel said. "We would yell, 'We're going to count three, and if you don't identify yourself, we're going to start shooting.'"

They could hear people fleeing.

During the days, the hurricane holdouts patrolled the streets protecting their houses and the ones of evacuees.

"I was packing," Robert Johns said. "A .22 magnum with hollow points and an 8 mm Mauser from World War II with armor-piercing shells."

Despite their efforts, some deserted houses in the neighborhood were broken into and looted, Pervel said.

Now the Algiers Point militia has defiantly declared it will not heed any orders for mandatory evacuation. The relatively elevated neighborhood area is across the Mississippi River from the city's worst flooded areas and has running water, gas and phone service.

"They say they're going to drag us kicking and screaming from our houses. For what? To take us to concentration camps where we'll be raped and killed," Ramona Parker said. "This is supposed to be America. We're honest citizens. We're not troublemakers. We pay our taxes."

"It would be cruel for the city to make us evacuate after what we've been through," Pervel said.

The roof was damaged on her house, and the rains left "water up to my ankles," Boza said. So she moved into her mother's home nearby.

She said she still has forty-two bullets to expend before she'll be forcibly evacuated.

"Then I hope the men they send to pull me out are six feet two inches and really cute," she said. "I'll be struggling and flirting at the same time."

The Funches Girls
of Post-Katrina New Orleans

Darkness has descended on the nearly deserted Ninth Ward as the Funches girls begin their nightly traipse down their front steps, along St. Claude Avenue, around the corner, to the FEMA trailer planted in the parking lot behind a funeral home.

"It's scary out here," says Sophia Funches, eight, as she and her seven-year-old sister, Olivia, carry a wicker basket filled with their carefully folded school clothes and backpacks and books for tomorrow.

Phyllis Funches strains to keep up with her daughters as they make their way down the banquette—which is what they call the sidewalk hereabouts—in their pajamas, robes and bedroom slippers. She lugs a gallon of milk for breakfast, Cheerios, and a laptop computer and a stack of files for late-night work on her job as an insurance adjuster.

"I'm tired like this every day. I'm just worn out," sighs Phyllis, thirty-seven, who has been divorced close to five years. "Come about seven o'clock, my forehead is sore. It's from holding my eyes open all day."

For Phyllis and others with lives still askew six months after Hurricane Katrina, their home town's nickname—the Big Easy—is a cruel reminder that nothing is ever easy now.

Although Katrina forever altered their hometown and their lives, the Funches (it rhymes with punches) family considers itself among the fortunate. They fled a day before the historic storm hit.

They returned to a house where raging wind blew off much of the roof but the rising floodwaters stopped inches before coming inside. The basement furnace was ruined. The roof and some ceilings and drywall must be replaced. Some rooms are uninhabitable. Hardwood floors must be sanded and refinished. New kitchen countertops will be needed. Hardest of all, reliable workers must be found.

But sleeping in the trailer provided by the Federal Emergency Management Agency while trying to repair their house, Phyllis says, "We're just inconvenienced."

They know stories of neighbors who died in the storm and its aftermath, houses that were demolished, schoolmates scattered to Lord knows where, relatives who lost jobs as well as homes, families that were separated, neighborhood stores that were looted, suffering that continues to this day.

No, the story of the Funches family is not the most tragic in New Orleans, a city where everyone has a sorrowful tale to tell six months into their post-K lives.

This is just one story of one family.

∼

Breakfast is served at 6:00 A.M. inside the cramped white trailer. Between spoonfuls of cereal and milk, Sophia and Olivia giggle about meeting a four-year-old neighborhood boy when they were living in Florida after escaping the storm.

"He asked Olivia if she wanted to see his thing," giggles Sophia.

"I said 'no' but he showed it anyway," Olivia giggles back.

It will not be the last time they experience bad behavior from a male, predicts their mom.

∼

Phyllis has never met her own father.

After the storm, she got a hankering to find him. She located his address on the Internet, but he was gone when she went there. Maybe it's for the best, she says.

"I don't think he knows I exist. Sometimes I think I'd like to go up to him and say 'How do.' But then, if he's the scum bucket I think he is, I wonder what's he going to want from me?"

Phyllis was born in the historic "Hotel Dieu" hospital—French for "House of God"—founded by the Catholic Sisters of Charity and turned over to the state in 1992. It has served as the first and last refuge for the poor.

Phyllis' mother went to high school two blocks from the house on St. Claude Avenue and moved to Mississippi when Phyllis was a baby. She mostly grew up there along with her sister, but New Orleans was fated to be the center of her life.

They moved back to New Orleans periodically and spent summers in the Crescent City with their maternal grandparents. After a year in junior college, Phyllis settled in New Orleans and became a cop, eventually reaching the rank of sergeant.

Some of her relatives disapproved when she married an African-American man, causing family rifts that have lingered past the divorce. Some kinfolks barely know her biracial daughters. "Funny because my grandmother is American Indian so she fully understands how it is to be shunned," Phyllis muses.

After a decade in blue, Phyllis left the New Orleans Police Department several years ago. She remembers investigating crimes and not knowing where the bullets were coming from in the shadows of the brick housing projects.

She got a job as a claims adjuster with Crawford & Company, a risk management firm, and has since doubled her police pay.

About thirteen years ago, she bought the house on St. Claude Avenue, which had been built in 1910 by a German immigrant. It has twelve-foot ceilings and wide beam floors and a front porch that oversees a display of decorated crosses that have been stuck on the neutral ground—the local term for a street median—since Katrina passed through.

"When we bought these houses, you couldn't give them away because of the neighborhood," she says.

But that was before the levees broke and left much of New Orleans under water.

"What stayed dry will gentrify," laughs Phyllis, quoting a newly minted real estate maxim.

~

Inside the maroon 2001 Toyota Camry with 209,922 miles on the odometer, Olivia and Sophia are wearing matching red Valentine's Day outfits with hearts on the front.

They are on the way to the Audubon Montessori School—a half-hour drive from home on a good traffic day. Olivia is one of seventeen students in Miss Beth's first grade class. Sophia is one of only ten in Mr. Tim's third grade class. The teachers' titles are traditionally Southern, as are the manners of the girls who are reminded often to say "yes sir" and "yes ma'am."

"This school was very hard to get in to and everyone wanted to go there," says Phyllis. But that was pre-Katrina.

Small class sizes and openings in an exclusive, yet free, magnet school are among the benefits of life in a city where most of the children have yet to return since the storm.

Thanks to cultural grants from around the country, Olivia is taking free ballet classes one afternoon a week while Sophia is learning to play the piano.

But driving her daughters across town to and from school takes a chunk of their mom's day. And her time is precious. She estimates that she has already processed 200 claims from the hurricane with no let-up in sight. Still, the car conversation on the school route is informative.

On their exodus after the storm, which included stops in nearly every Gulf Coast state, the family spent one night in an emergency facility in Chipley, Florida.

"I loved the Red Cross center. Olivia and I didn't want to leave," says Sophia. "They had junk food and television and beds."

But then there was that strange man sleeping right next to them. "He snored real loud," remembers Olivia, scrunching her face at the memory.

~

The girls stayed with family friends in Gainesville, Florida, and attended school there when Phyllis first returned to their house in the fall. There was no electricity in New Orleans then, of course, and she chased down Salvation Army trucks to get canned chicken and saltines for suppers. Using propane fuel in the yard, she heated water in the crawfish pot for baths.

Winston Leer, who lives nearby, stayed through the storm. He saw the looters go through the corner store owned by a Vietnamese couple and watched the helicopters unload rescued people down the street. Winston survived on military Meals-Ready-To-Eat, or MREs, and on appropriated beer, Phyllis says, judging from the empty packages in his yard.

She brought her daughters home over the Christmas holidays and they started in the new school on January 3. Every other weekend, Sophia and Olivia visit their dad in Lake Charles Parish.

On those weekends, Phyllis often heads out of town to investigate claims that are more than a day's drive away. The girls have gone with her on other weekend work trips to Texas.

"I'll be working claims on this freaking storm through May," she believes. Then another hurricane season begins.

Meanwhile, mundane has disappeared from her lexicon.

Making groceries—what folks here say when they shop for food— used to be simple for the Funches. Now it requires a trip across the Mississippi River to the West Bank. There are still no stores open near their house.

Phyllis makes a list for a visit to a Target store: "Toilet Paper. Soap Powder. Wrinkle Stuff. Coffee. Color Pencils. V-Day Cards. Hair Jell. Printer Cartridges." It takes a two-hour trip to buy these items and return home after picking up the girls at school.

There is still no mail delivery in their neighborhood. Phyllis has the important correspondence sent to Café Rose Nicaud. "We always read it first," jokes the woman behind the counter. Phyllis also did her computer work at the café before her electricity was restored and now returns there whenever it is lost again.

"Oh, the power goes out every five days or so," she says.

In the trailer, the hot water lasts four and a half minutes. "You make sure you are good and naked before you get in that shower," she says.

It is a strange, split existence that will only get more complicated as work begins on their house and they can spend less time there. She has hired roofers who came from Missouri for the plentiful jobs, as well as carpenters from Illinois, and hopes a friend from the café can help with painting. But desperate homeowners and business people all over southeast Louisiana are bidding on workers, so when or whether they show up is a mystery.

Meanwhile, the girls sleep together on an upper bunk in the trailer. But signs still hang on the doorknobs of their bedrooms in the house. "Sophia F.—Olivia Can Not Come In, Only Mom," says one. "Jesus Loves You and So Do I," says the other.

After the storm, any guideposts and traditions that survived are cherished.

As always, Phyllis put green, gold and purple Mardi Gras bunting on the front door. Only now the decorations are next to a wall that is spray painted with symbolic reminders of Katrina. The "9/12" shows the day rescue workers came to the house and the "NE" stands for "No Entry." The "0" means the rescue workers saw no bodies when they peered through the windows.

~

It is almost time to go to the FEMA trailer. But Olivia has to make a model Mardi Gras float for tomorrow's class and her mom and sister are helping out. Fussing and laughing, they use hot glue to stick green, gold and purple construction paper to a box and affix a back and decorative crowns. The project is proclaimed fit for a miniature parade. Sophia and Olivia bathe and change into pajamas while Phyllis goes back to her computer.

Then, sleepy-eyed, all three set out for the trailer. Another day is done.

Their lives may never be what they were before Katrina arrived. But the Funches girls are together again. And they know that's what matters most.

Fat Tuesday in the Big Uneasy

Under a sunny blue sky, the people came out to celebrate the first Fat Tuesday since Hurricane Katrina belied the nickname of their beloved hometown—the Big Easy.

Mardi Gras 2006. It was a day like the happy old times—not the recent hard ones—a day to once again let the good times roll.

Zulu—the African-American "krewe" or Mardi Gras club—paraded past houses still spray-painted with the dates they were searched for bodies—dead or alive—and bearing the numbers and symbols of the results.

Afterward, Zulu members strutted in a symbolic "Second Line" behind a jazz band in memory of the ten fellow krewemen who died in the storm and its aftermath.

"We needed some return of normalcy," said Rene Baigle, who was wearing a shiny gold workman's hard hat atop her purple wig and a tool belt with plastic hammer, screwdriver, wrench and saw.

Her husband, Sparke Edwards, was outfitted in a grass skirt, a cape made from a blue tarp with "Wasted Away In FEMA-ville" on the back and a lei made of MRE packets.

Both are physicians.

They watched the Zulu parade on Jackson Avenue, across from a house that had burned since the storm but bore a sign saying, "I am coming home. I will rebuild. I am New Orleans."

"I wonder sometimes if the rest of the country wonders, 'What are those idiots doing down there having Mardi Gras?" said Dr. Baigle, who lives in Baton Rouge and at one time had fourteen friends who had fled Katrina staying in her house. "But this is normal for us. We needed this."

Normalcy indeed. A prime position in the French Quarter belonged to Frank Morton, Jr., a defensive tackle at Tulane University who was working as a bouncer at Mango Mango Daquiris.

His seat was beneath a balcony full of beads droppers and a few feet away from where a succession of young women were baring their breasts for souvenir necklaces on Bourbon Street.

Inside a cardboard model of a refrigerator wrapped with duct tape was Kathryn Rogers, a five-months-pregnant textbook editor from Austin, Texas.

"This is the most important Mardi Gras of my life so far," said Rogers, 36, who grew up in New Orleans and has been attending Carnival almost since birth. "I would not have missed this."

She was a member of the impromptu "Krewe de Phew" whose outfits recalled the odor of food that spoiled inside of refrigerators that were thrown on the streets after the storm. They paraded on foot through the French Quarter.

Pre-teen girls had (hopefully temporarily) dyed their hair purple, green and gold—Mardi Gras colors.

Along Jackson Avenue, the Zulu parade passed by signs nailed to power poles. "We Buy Houses. Cash...Fast!" "Gutting, Painting, Drywall and More."

Geneva Robertson watched from a folding chair with her FEMA number on the back—signifying her place in a line for help that has never come.

"We just about finished fixing our house now," she said. "We could hardly get FEMA on the phone, much less get a trailer from them."

Her family has lived upstairs above a flooded beauty parlor since the storm.

When you lose possessions, she said, "you realize that life is what is important and the love everyone has shown."

She was in her seat three hours before the parade began. "From when I was a child, I have loved Mardi Gras," she said.

Mardi Gras was a gumbo of music:

The fiddle and accordion of Cajun music from speakers on the back of a pick-up. Rap from houses along the Zulu route. Dixieland from a band leading a strutting "Second Line" of costumed celebrants in the French Quarter. Country blasting from the Bourbon Cowboy on Bourbon Street. Marches from high school bands in parades. Jazz from a guy who played the trumpet for tips and sang in a Louis Armstrong rasp on the sidewalk by Café du Monde. Raunchy rock providing background noise for women—or what looked like them—enticing customers for dance performances.

The sounds never stopped.

All along St. Charles Avenue, children in costumes watched the parades perched in boxes atop ladders.

"You hate it when they outgrow the box seats," said a nostalgic mom. "Then you have to worry about them running around everywhere."

Wearing his full feathered regalia, Ivory Holmes was searching for other members of the Golden Comanches, his neighborhood tribe of Mardi Gras Indians. These clubs, made up mostly of African Americans, gather early on Fat Tuesday and dance through the area, picking up other tribes as they go, explained Holmes, whose tribal name is "Wild Man."

His house was flooded but his elaborately beaded Indian costume was spared, he said, "because I had it up on a mannikin and the water couldn't get to it."

Now, though, he was seeking but not finding other Golden Comanches who had come out for the parade.

"I lost everything but I'm still here," he said. "It's a tradition."

The colors and costumes came at you fast:

A purple, green and gold suit and matching cap made entirely of plastic doubloons thrown from Mardi Gras parades. It took Dave Roberts close to three years to collect the 780 doubloons on the suit, which he managed to save despite having to evacuate to Atlanta, where he and his wife had lived in the mid-1990s.

"We're back here to stay—until the next one hits," he promised.

Ron Canedo wore a white jump suit smeared with green gobs of paint. His companion, Ann Rogers, was decked out in an evening gown and lots of sparkle.

"The Mold and the Beautiful." Get it?

The Mardi Gras float titled "Hurling" rolled down Canal Street carrying a giant model of a discarded refrigerator with the door held shut by faux adhesive tape.

Adorned with beads and watching from the sidewalk, savvy survivors of the odorous aftermath of Hurricane Katrina chuckled knowingly at this festive remembrance of regurgitation.

"I cleaned out eight refrigerators" filled with rotten food in the weeks after the storm, recalled Blake Bascle, identifying with the "Hurling" float's brightly painted cartoon characters depicted in the act.

"I lived a block behind the fish market," one-upped his parade-watching companion, Kenny Zeiger.

From a fashion show featuring designer creations made from the blue tarpaulins that still cover many damaged roofs to parades with satirical themes like "Rode Hard and Put Up Wet," folks in this flood-fatigued city are using Mardi Gras to poke fun at their troubles.

"It's not to say we don't understand the seriousness of our situation, but sometimes you have to laugh in order not to cry," said Mardi Gras historian Arthur Hardy. "Mardi Gras is group therapy for us."

A clinical psychologist agreed.

The parade of pointed humor, which outsiders might view as odd in a city still crippled six months after being hit by the historic storm, "is a remarkably good sign of healing," said Steven Sultanoff, past president of the Association for Applied and Therapeutic Humor.

"When individuals are able to laugh at themselves in crisis, it shows emotional resolution of stress. Not that the stress is completely gone, but it shows that one is now in the recovery stage," explained Sultanoff, who practices in California and teaches psychology at Pepperdine University.

Tastewise, not much short of death and injury is off limits in this comedy club of a Carnival.

The Knights of Chaos, one of the "krewes" or private clubs that put on the Mardi Gras parades, rolled out a float called "The Inferno." It portrays Mayor Ray Nagin, Louisiana Gov. Kathleen Blanco and former Federal Emergency Management Agency Director Michael Brown sporting devil horns and cooking a gumbo filled with the people of New Orleans in a cauldron that resembles an upside-down Superdome.

The Chaos float "Chocolate Divinity" used a white figure scalding in hot chocolate to recall Nagin's infamous prediction that New Orleans would emerge from rebuilding as "a chocolate city."

The krewe's "Corpse of Engineers" float featured construction plans for a levee that begin with a layer of iron as a building material, then has layers of mud, peat and Jell-O before ending up in Hades.

Faced with the actual events and painfully slow recovery, said Chaos member Ted Kennedy, "What else are you going to do but laugh?"

That was certainly the spirit behind the Krewe of Mid-City parade, with its theme of "Rode Hard and Put Up Wet" and floats titled "Survivor ... New Orleans Style," "MRE Meal," "Refrigerator Heaven," "Drove My Chevy to the Levee but the Levee Was Gone," and "New Orleans Culture," starring the mold growing in so many sodden houses.

There was a Krewe of Muses float depicting the confrontation on a bridge where Gretna police blocked fleeing New Orleans residents, many of them black, from entering their mostly white suburb. It is shown as a child's game: "Red Rover, Red Rover, We Won't Let (You) Come Over."

Another float by the all-female Muses satirized the finger-pointing between government officials. It has Nagin singing a version of the Shirley Ellis '60s song "The Name Game." But in the Mardi Gras "Blame Game," the lyrics go, "Blanco! Blanco, Blanco bo anco, banana fanna fo Flanco. Fee fi mo Manco. Blanco!"

"We have to laugh. We've been through so much," said parade-watcher Alexis DeBram.

But it takes time to achieve "the emotional separation" for survivors to see humor in their predicaments, said Sultanoff, the psychologist.

"We laugh at our stories now, but it wasn't funny five and six months ago," agreed DeBram.

For example, the Krewe du Vieux parade's theme is "C'est Levee," a pun on the French phrase "c'est la vie" or "that's life." The play on words would not have seemed so witty to those waiting to be rescued on a Ninth Ward roof after the levees were breached.

Mardi Gras parades have a tradition of timely humor, said Hardy, author of the annual "Mardi Gras Guide" and a book on the history of the New Orleans Carnival.

"In 1873, parades made fun of the carpetbaggers in Reconstruction," ridiculing the transplanted Yankees in power after the Civil War, said Hardy. "Everybody gets lampooned."

A defiant 2006 Mardi Gras doubloon said it all: "Come Hell Or High Water."

It would take more than the worst natural disaster in United States history to stop this party.

Strings of plastic beads and strains of Dixieland music filled the air. Gargantuan faces smiled down from passing floats as sidewalks turned into rivers of hands reaching up for gaudy trinkets. The crowds— although smaller than normal—were grateful that Mardi Gras 2006 had begun less than six months since hurricanes laid waste to their city.

"All along the way, we saw people holding up signs saying 'Thanks for parading'," said Wayne Cucullu, who rode on a satirical Roman idol float depicting "FEMA—God of the Sea in Our Living Rooms."

Well-wishers came from around the country to join festivities in a city whose tragedies they had watched for weeks on television.

"After Katrina, we had to come and show our support for the city," said Crystal Pinson, a stay-at-home mom from Douglasville, Georgia, who was holding her bead-laden eleven son, Prior.

"My husband grew up here and we had to see how his old neighborhood made out," said Crystal.

So how did it make out?

"Not too well, actually," said her husband, Chris Pinson, who attended his first Mardi Gras at the age of two months. Although the home of his aunt and uncle survived intact, many of the neighboring houses on Lake Pontchartrain did not.

The losses suffered by the city were not reflected in any shortage of Mardi Gras beads, however, judging from the sack full carried by Megan Pinson, a ten-year-old fourth grader.

"I love it," she declared, grinning with a face painted in purple and gold.

The notion of having a huge party only a few miles from where whole neighborhoods are still demolished and deserted did not strike the early revelers as odd.

"They had to have Mardi Gras," said Phyllis Abadie, a New Orleans native who came from Holt, Florida, on what is an annual party pilgrimage.

But life in New Orleans now is strange, admitted her son, Ron Blum, a Tulane University law student.

"If you have a kid who needs medicine at 10:30 at night, you're out of luck," he said. "But if you need a gin and tonic, there are a multitude of places to go and get one."

The parades are paid for by krewes, or private clubs, like Rex and Sparta whose members buy or rent floats and hire the artists whose creations depict a new theme each year. Masked and costumed krewe members ride on their floats and throw out the plastic beads and fake coins that commemorate their organization and Mardi Gras 2006.

Membership costs vary by krewe, of course. In Bacchus, for example, the initiation fee is $500 and annual dues are $750, said Owen Brennan III, the krewe's executive director and a member of the family that owns several restaurants in the French Quarter.

Bacchus, one of the so-called Super Krewes with 1,200 members and thirty-two floats, is widely credited with helping change Mardi Gras in New Orleans from a regional Carnival into an international tourist destination.

In the late 1940s, "Mardi Gras was a closed event. If you weren't born into a krewe, you could watch the parades but not participate," said Brennan. Then his grandfather, the first Owen Brennan, and other New Orleans business owners founded Bacchus—named for the Roman god of wine and revelry and open to the public for membership.

Bacchus came up with the concept of a celebrity Mardi Gras king—this year's is Michael Keaton—and over the years brought in folks like Jackie Gleason, Bob Hope and Charlton Heston to reign over their parade.

Other Super Krewes were organized and Mardi Gras was transformed. Although no commercialization is allowed on the floats, the parades "are very business oriented," said Brennan.

Most krewes allow substitutions for riders, for instance, so members can invite clients and bosses to dress up and throw out beads in a once-in-a-lifetime Mardi Gras parade.

While the floats offer a great view of female parade watchers flashing their breasts for souvenir bead throws, the rituals are important to the krewes.

Some of the organizations videotape the procession from unannounced spots along the route, said Errol Laborde, author of two books on Mardi Gras and editor of New Orleans Magazine.

"If members are caught on tape with their masks off," he said, "they're kicked out of the krewe."

Indeed, it is illegal to ride on a float in a Mardi Gras parade without wearing a costume and mask.

"It's the law," said Laborde, citing a city ordinance.

He said it is hard to exaggerate the significance of this annual event on the history, culture and economy of the Crescent City.

"And this is the most important Mardi Gras ever," said the historian.

But also the most bipolar.

Debauchery and Destruction. Revelry and Rebirth. Celebration and Closure. The French Quarter was filled with partiers and there were waits for tables at landmark restaurants like K-Paul's Louisiana Kitchen. Meanwhile, tourists lined up for the Grey Line Devastation Tour to see where the levees were breached and view deserted houses still in shambles in the lower Ninth Ward and Lakeside.

"We have lost our loved ones. We have lost some of our communities, our jobs, our homes," said Angele Davis, Louisiana's Secretary of Culture, Recreation and Tourism.

"It's a hard time for us. But we have to rebuild. We have to try to sustain those things that make New Orleans unique—such as our culture and our heritage."

Mardi Gras springs from the very soul of the city of Satchmo and second-line strutters trailing the casket in a funeral procession and lazy breakfasts of beignets and cafe au lait, say the wearers of Carnival colors of purple, green and gold.

"We came so close to really knowing what it means to miss New Orleans, explained Sandra Shilstone, president of the New Orleans Tourism Marketing Corporation.

But off the crowded streets, there was another Mardi Gras.

"There is a private side to Carnival. It started as an event that we did for ourselves and it still is," said Arthur Hardy, the Mardi Gras historian.

"The economic side is monumental and it's good for the city. But we chose to do this for us."

"The city government could have canceled this event, but they couldn't have put it on. That takes the people" to accomplish, said Hardy.

Indeed, few tourists—desperately wooed by this cash-strapped city for the first post-Katrina Mardi Gras—ventured far enough along St. Charles Avenue to hear the Dixieland band and see storm survivors strut in the front-yard party of the extended Landrieu family.

For kin and friends who have been scattered by storm and consumed with rebuilding their houses and lives, the gathering is like a reunion, said Phyllis Landrieu, the hostess and aunt of Sen. Mary Landrieu, D-La., and Louisiana Lieutenant Governor Mitch Landrieu. "Miss Phyllis" herself is president of the Orleans Parish School Board.

As usual, the Landrieu party began Saturday and continued virtually nonstop through Fat Tuesday. It concluded at midnight when Lenten sacrifice begins on Ash Wednesday.

"Welcome," proclaimed Miss Phyllis, hugging an arrival. "Thank goodness you're here."

Many weren't there, of course, as more than half of New Orleans' pre-Katrina populace of 465,000 had not returned since being displaced by the storms. But thousands of families that have come back, camped out on the sidewalks and "neutral ground"—the local term for a street median—and watched the parades from traditional spots a seeming world away from the TV cameras, boisterous bars and women who flashed their breasts for beads.

David Landrieu cooked up a pot of Oysters Rockefeller Soup on his mama's driveway. "Everybody brings a dish," explained Miss Phyllis.

"For six months we have been so busy rebuilding that we haven't had a chance to get together," said Shilstone "Now that Mardi Gras is here, we're having a homecoming."

A Year Afterward

The heavy heat of August has returned to New Orleans, and Miss Jeanetta dabs at perspiration with a tissue as she sits in the scant shade and recalls her Katrina odyssey.

Almost a year has passed since rescue workers in boats pulled Jeanetta DeCou and 10 family members from her attic while floodwaters engulfed the very porch where she now tells her story.

"It's a lot better than any of us thought it would be," said Miss Jeanetta, who personifies the ordeal that her beloved hometown is still struggling to overcome.

A year after the greatest natural disaster in American history, every house—some reoccupied, many still in shambles—has a story to tell in this sweltering city where the levees failed.

In a place where 160,000 homes were destroyed or heavily damaged after Hurricane Katrina arrived August 29, 2005, recovery has often been about both perseverance and location.

When their Gentilly Terrace neighborhood was flooded, the DeCou family was deposited by rescue boats onto Interstate-10. They had only the clothes they were wearing, a few bottles of water, crackers and tins of Vienna sausage. Even Mimi, the family dog, was left in the attic.

They slept on concrete for three nights as they walked to the convention center, where Miss Jeanetta found her eighty-nine-year-old mother and a rolling office chair to push her around in.

After five days of fear and filth, they were loaded onto a bus, taken to the airport and flown to Corpus Christi, where Miss Jeanetta's brother took in their mother and the DeCous began a disjointed journey home.

A daughter and two sons went to Atlanta. Some grandchildren ended up in Arkansas. Miss Jeanetta went to Dallas; to Houma, Louisiana; to a sister's house across the Mississippi River from New Orleans in Algiers; to her mother's house nearby; and, finally, on Mother's Day, to a Federal Emergency Management Agency trailer in her front yard, where she still lives.

"I had to come home," she said. "This is my house. This is my neighborhood. This is where I belong."

She is reminded of those sweaty, scary nights on the freeway as she rides a bus to work each day, passing places where she saw corpses. She counts her blessings.

Even Mimi, her grandson's pet, was saved. The dog was taken to Arizona by volunteer rescuers. Miss Jeanetta's mother is back after praying, "Lord, please don't let me die in Texas."

But neither of Miss Jeanetta's next-door neighbors has returned.

Mostly ghosts live in the Lower Ninth Ward, where head-high weeds have replaced the fetid waters that rose to the roofs. A faded green clapboard house remains atop a white Chevrolet Prizm near the corner of Lizardi and Law streets. Many blocks are still without water or electricity.

In similarly hard-hit New Orleans East, fewer than twenty percent of the 90,000 residents have returned, according to a study from the Brookings Institution, a Washington think tank. In Lakeview, where waters from the 17th Street Canal gushed through a breached levee, only a tiny fraction of families are back.

But in the French Quarter and along scenic St. Charles Avenue, where damage came from wind rather than water, almost everyone has returned.

On high-standing Bourbon Street in the French Quarter, bar bands blast away nightly, and festive pedestrians carry potent rum Hurricane drinks or huge cups of beer.

On a commercial strip of St. Bernard Avenue in the low-lying suburb of Chalmette, which was flooded after the storm hit, there are no pedestrians. Charlie's Barber Shop, Ken's Tropical Fish, Campiere Custom Design, A-1 Lock and Key and every other business remain closed.

Although population estimates vary, the latest New Orleans telephone book documents the decline of a city. There are 100,000 fewer names in the white pages than were listed before Katrina, and the yellow pages are in the same volume rather than in a separate book.

Michael Tisserand, former editor of the Big Easy's alternative newspaper, Gambit Weekly, is among those who left. The emotional decision to move to Illinois still haunts him.

"New Orleans is a unique and wonderful place," he said.

His job and house survived the hurricane, but the medical practice of his wife, a pediatrician, collapsed. The physician with whom she had worked committed suicide after the storm.

The depressed doctor "was a model New Orleanian to us. He made the most amazing Mardi Gras costumes and always helped the community," Tisserand said.

But the doctor's office and house were flooded, Tisserand said, and "he couldn't see his way out."

The labor force in metropolitan New Orleans is about thirty percent smaller than it was a year ago, the Brookings Institution reported. The area lost about 190,000 workers and now has about 444,000.

Yolanda Evans, who spent most of the past year in Riverdale, Georgia, with friends and family, decided to return even though her job with the city's Office of Community Services is shaky.

"Rebuilding will be slow," she said. "But I want to be part of the future of New Orleans."

Evans is conflicted about where to live, however. And her situation illustrates the complexity of resettlement for thousands of families.

Her brick house in the Oak Island subdivision of New Orleans East could be repaired, but at considerable cost. Only a handful of houses in the sprawling development have been reoccupied.

"I don't want to invest all my money into rebuilding my house and then have the neighborhood never come back," said Evans, who has a twenty-two-year-old son and a ten-year-old daughter. "But both of my children were raised here. This is the only home they've ever known."

After having the house gutted, she returned to find that someone had stolen the toilet and bathtub. She is now living in a FEMA trailer in the backyard of her father's house. Her father lives in a FEMA trailer in the front.

"Some people are negative about the recovery, but I only want to talk to the positive ones," Evans said. "I made my decision to come back, and I don't want to second-guess myself."

Kiki and Derek Huston, whose children attend the Robert Mills Lusher School with Evans' daughter, Diamond, are among the optimists.

But while Evans drives her child across the city to the independently run charter school that emphasizes the arts, the Hustons walk there with Olivia, ten, and Walker, seven, in the Carrollton neighborhood, which was largely spared by Katrina.

Their neighborhood is part of the "sliver by the river," which includes the French Quarter and Garden District. The floodwaters stopped at their doorstep, Derek Huston said.

Many of the neighbors evacuated together, he said, and set up a school they dubbed "the Sugar Cane Academy" in the agricultural community of New Iberia.

He plays the saxophone in a roots rock band called the Iguanas, and several of the band members fled to Austin.

"Most of the gigs we had were on the road" during that time, he said. The perceptions of people outside New Orleans ranged from sympathy to bewilderment about why someone would want to live below sea level in a city protected by levees that had already proved to be unreliable.

"It's a bizarre feeling when you have to justify to other people about where you live," he said, pleading for patience from the nation. It took centuries to make New Orleans what it was before Katrina, he said. It may take decades to rebuild it.

The number of students in New Orleans has fallen from about 60,000 before Katrina to about 20,000 this fall. About fifty-four schools will open, compared with about 100 before Katrina.

But seats are full at Le Chat Noir, a theater where the sold-out solo cabaret show "I'm Still Here, Me!" has been held over.

Actor Ricky Graham plays a host of post-Katrina characters—Bitsy Chardonnay, the socialite survivor; Mr. Otto, the Ninth Ward fixer forced to live in his mother's house—as New Orleans proves again that it is a city that can laugh at its troubles.

When asked about signs of recovery, one young mom in the Garden District marveled: "You can find baby sitters."

Bayou Doc

Shafts of light from the setting sun sparkle on the bayou as Dr. Regina Benjamin drives her blue Toyota pick-up along the two-lane black-top to a house call in the piney woods.

The left big toe of a toothless, bedridden old man has turned black with infection. After examination, the doctor prescribes a powerful antibiotic.

Home visits were part of her practice even before Hurricane Katrina ripped through this Gulf Coast fishing village, leaving houses and businesses in ruins and forcing folks into FEMA trailers and relatives' homes.

"It's hard for their families to get them back and forth from the doctor's office," says Benjamin, forty-nine, explaining the need to go out to her patients.

She greets the start of another storm season with a shrug.

Hurricanes come and go hereabouts. But there are always neighbors needing care in this sweltering backwater community whose brief brush with fame came as a locale in the movie "Forrest Gump."

The doctor, a devoted daughter of this unforgiving region of marshes and miseries, has stayed despite possessing skill and a reputation that could garner riches elsewhere. For instance, she was the first African-American woman to serve on the American Medical Association Board of Trustees.

"Dr. Benjamin has been a blessing to this community," said Mayor Stan Wright, a part-time politician as apt to be found at his family oyster house as at City Hall. "It wouldn't surprise me if I saw her coming up the road in a goat cart if that's the only way she could reach a patient. If you don't have money to pay her, just bring her a pint of oysters and she's happy."

"She's a real doctor. That's the bottom line," said the mayor, who mentions with a bit of pride that he is among her patients. Her office is a double-wide trailer now. Air-conditioned, it is a medical oasis compared to the steamy stage at a community center where she treated hundreds of patients in the weeks immediately after the storm flooded her clinic.

That facility had been built on high ground after Hurricane Georges destroyed her first storefront office near the drawbridge into town in 1998. The second clinic was purposefully situated in a spot that had never been flooded in the bayou's recorded history.

The twenty-five-foot tidal surge from Katrina left it completely submerged.

But perhaps the cruelest blow was still undelivered.

Beginning in the early days of last September, the clinic staff spread medical records in the sun to dry and villagers and volunteers from elsewhere pitched in to rebuild the clinic. They worked for months while Benjamin practiced out of the trailer and her pick-up. By Christmas, the records and medicines and equipment had been moved back in and the facility was set to reopen as the new year began.

On January 1, 2006, the rebuilt Bayou La Batre Rural Health Clinic burned down. The fire was so hot that the front of the nearby trailer melted. The cause has not been determined.

Dr. Regina Benjamin, of course, remains nothing but determined.

Deborah Williamson, a waitress at Uncle Trey's restaurant on the Dauphin Island Parkway, has come to see the doctor about her headaches. The pain could be caused by stress, she reckons, from fretting about the future after losing her house to Katrina.

"It's a big change going from a big house to a little-bitty ol' (FEMA) trailer," she explains. "I think it's worse on my husband than on me. He's really got cabin fever."

They can't rebuild their old house because it was in a flood zone and can't find a new house that they can afford.

"It's hard starting over at fifty," says Williamson.

Patients have been taking their ailments and woes to "Dr. B" since before she officially opened the doors to her private practice in 1990. She was nailing up sheetrock in an office full of sawdust when the first one showed up—a young woman with a sick baby. Putting down the hammer, she treated the child. There has been no let-up since.

Bayou La Batre is home to 2,315 people, a third of whom are of Vietnamese descent. Nearly all the jobs are in the seafood industry and medical insurance is rare—especially among those who go out on shrimp boats and would have to pay increased premiums because of their high-risk occupations.

"They're hardworking people," said Mayor Wright. "They've come up the hard way and that's the only way they know."

Many balk at free medical care subsidized by the government. So Benjamin wanted to set up a practice that fit the needs and sentiments of the community.

"I wanted to allow people to keep their dignity so I let them pay what they can when they can pay it," she declares. She recalls a shrimper who paid $5 a week over two bad seasons before plunking down cash to pay off his $1,000-plus account after a bountiful one.

"They work for a living and they're proud," she says.

Regina Benjamin grew up in nearby Daphne. Her parents separated when she was two. Her mother was a waitress and her father was a government worker who followed his job to the West Coast. Both died in recent years.

Asked what in her childhood inspired her to be a doctor, she bluntly replies, "Nothing."

"I had never seen a black doctor before I went to college," she recalled.

At Xavier University in New Orleans, she majored in chemistry and joined the pre-med club. Following graduation, she enrolled in the Morehouse School of Medicine in Atlanta. Dr. Louis Sullivan, who would become Secretary of Health and Human Services, was dean at the time.

"David Satcher taught me community medicine," she recalled. "He would take us out to all these little towns in Georgia."

This same David Satcher would go on to become Director of the Centers for Disease Control and Prevention in Atlanta and Surgeon General of the United States.

After completing her medical education at the University of Alabama at Birmingham's School of Medicine and subsequent residency, the new physician worked several years at a regional clinic outside Bayou La Batre before setting up her private practice.

She quickly discovered that she knew little of the economics of being the only doctor in a poor fishing village. So she augmented her income by moonlighting at hospital emergency rooms in Mobile, and her knowledge by commuting to New Orleans to earn an MBA from Tulane University.

"The main reason I got an MBA was that I wanted to figure out how to provide cost-effective medical care to people who can't afford" treatment financed by insurance or the government, she said.

"I'm still trying to learn that," she admits.

Across the water from the docks, shrimp boats still rest high and dry amid the trees where Katrina deposited them nine months ago. The devastating storm left 2,000 of the town's 2,315 residents homeless.

"I couldn't find my patients at first. They had all left their homes," said Benjamin. So she set up shop on the community center stage and took care of the stream of displaced people and relief workers who came for treatment. Luckily, a drug store survived beyond the high water mark.

"I told the pharmacist to bill me for prescriptions," she said. "I saw patients for free and didn't start billing until March."

A fund set up by Charles Barkley, the former NBA basketball player and an Alabama native, eventually paid for most of the medicines, she said.

Since Katrina, the close-knit community has become closer.

Inside the double-wide, patients and staff inquire about the well-being of each other and relatives.

"How is your mama?" receptionist Cyndi Clark asks Lisa Willis, a poet and shipbuilder whose mother is also a patient.

Willis brought a poem for Clark, whose father died recently, and wrote a Mother's Day poem for the doctor, in honor of Benjamin's late mother.

"I trust Dr. B," said Willis, when asked why she comes here for care.

Martin Hernandez, a shrimper more comfortable speaking Spanish than English, comes in complaining that he is thirsty and urinating all the time. A blood test shows highly elevated sugar levels. Diabetes is suspected. He is already being treated by Benjamin for high blood pressure.

"She still don't send me no bills," marvels Hernandez. "You know how it is, other places they send you a big bill."

Nell Stoddard, the seventy-six-year-old nurse, explains about insulin and teaches Hernandez to give himself injections, just in case. He works on a boat that goes out in the Gulf for two weeks at a time.

"I've only been doing this for fifty years," says the white-haired "Miss Nell."

It is the first day in the trailer for two students from Atlanta's Morehouse medical school who are here to "shadow" Benjamin. With stethoscopes ready around their necks, Keimun Slaughter, whose parents live in Marietta, Georgia, and Nick Borm, whose parents in live in Alpharetta, Georgia, are wide-eyed at a medical practice that seems straight from Mayberry.

The patients really open up to Benjamin, observes Slaughter. "You don't see that in Atlanta."

Someone asks what time the trailer closes.

"Whenever we finish with the last patient," answers Clark.

A SENSE OF PLACE

~

An Ear to the Sky   *Photo by Rick McKay*

Remembering D-Day Every Day

Weeks of waves had washed the blood from the beaches of Normandy before townsfolk learned how D-Day had devastated their peaceful community in the shadow of the Blue Ridge Mountains.

It was July of 1944. Elizabeth Teass was working in the telegraph booth in the back of Green's Drug Store when the warning from the Roanoke operator clicked out on the teletype machine: "I have casualties."

Green's was a lively place back then. The stools at the soda fountain were nearly always occupied. In the mornings, businessmen came in for coffee and gossip. High school kids slurped milkshakes and flirted away the afternoons. But on that July day the chatter stopped cold.

The telegrams came one after the other until the town thought they would never stop. Each expressed the "deep regret" of the Secretary of War. Over the next week, Bedford would learn that twenty-one of its sons had died on June 6, 1944, in the D-Day invasion of France.

Amid a populace of 3,200, "if you didn't know the person who had been killed, you probably knew his family," recalled Elizabeth Teass, who was twenty-one that summer.

There were so many telegrams that Sheriff Jim Marshall enlisted the undertaker and taxi driver to help deliver them to parents and wives in town and on surrounding farms.

But it was the husky sheriff himself who went to the Hoback dairy farm. The family was about to go to services at the Center Point Methodist Church, which was just across the road, the first time Marshall stood awkwardly on the porch and delivered his news. Pvt. Bedford Hoback, thirty, had been killed on D-Day.

A day or so later, the two teen-aged Hoback sisters were churning ice cream to try to comfort their grieving parents when the sheriff returned. Staff Sergeant Raymond Hoback, twenty-four, was missing in action. Later, Bedford men who did return from the war remembered a wounded Raymond waiting on Omaha Beach to be transported back to a ship. They theorized that he drowned when the tide came in. His body was never found.

Her parents were never the same after those telegrams, said Lucille Hoback Boggess, who was fifteen that sad summer.

Afterward, her mother wouldn't go on family picnics and such. It was as if she thought that she shouldn't enjoy herself if her sons weren't there to have fun, too. And their father would send the sisters from the dinner table whenever they were laughing, Boggess said.

On every Bedford street, it seemed, there was a house with a gold star in the window.

A whole town was in mourning for a lost generation.

～

On a dusty construction site on the edge of Bedford, the granite arch of the National D-Day Memorial rises forty-four feet and six inches above the Victory Plaza inlaid with the Allied designation for the five Normandy beaches: Omaha. Utah. Gold. Sword. Juno. The height symbolizes the invasion date: 6/6/44. The word "Overlord" is emblazoned on the arch. "Operation Overlord" was the code name for the Normandy landing.

On Memorial Day, this first phase of the National D-Day Memorial—the arch and plaza—will be opened to the public. The completed project, including an adjoining education center, is scheduled to be dedicated on June 6, 2001, the fifty-seventh anniversary of the historic landing that is now remembered as the turning point of World War

II. Although funded mostly by private donations, the $12.2 million memorial was approved by Congress in 1996 to honor the valor and sac-rifices of the 175,000 Allied forces involved in the invasion.

The Allies suffered 9,758 casualties on D-Day, including 6,603 from the United States. This rural community by a bend in the Little Otter River was chosen for the national memorial because it experienced the greatest per-capita loss of any American town or city. Of the thirty-five sons of Bedford who landed at Normandy, nineteen died within the first fifteen minutes of the battle and two more were lost later during that longest day.

The Bedford casualties were all members of an activated Virginia National Guard unit, the 116th Infantry Regiment of the 29th Division. Along with regular army units from the First Infantry Division, these were the first soldiers to go ashore at Omaha Beach, scene of some of the bloodiest fighting. The companies of the 116th Regiment went ashore alphabetically—and Bedford was the home of Company A.

~

The Stevens twins, Roy and Ray, were platoon sergeants in Company A. They had grown up on a farm outside of Bedford and were inseparable from boyhood. They were together when their National Guard unit steamed to England aboard the Queen Mary and they bunked in the same barracks during training for the invasion.

But on D-Day, they headed ashore in separate Higgins Landing Craft with their different platoons.

They agreed to meet at an intersection on the map. "Ray wanted me to shake his hand" upon departure, Roy recalls. "But I said we would shake when we met up at that crossroads."

In the cold, choppy channel, though, the boat carrying Roy Stevens' platoon hit an underwater German obstacle and sank. Most of those aboard managed to stay afloat for several hours until being picked up and taken back to England. Four days would pass before Roy Stevens landed on Omaha Beach. There was already a row of fresh graves.

The first wooden cross he examined was marked with the dog tag of his twin brother.

"After I saw Ray's grave, I said 'I'm going to get even' and I volunteered for everything to try to get some revenge," he recalled. "But twenty days was all that I had in battle. It seemed like an eternity."

Out on patrol, he was wounded by an exploding land mine. After surgery and a stay in a field hospital, he spent the remainder of the war in England training soldiers to be sent to the front.

Then came V-E Day and he went home to Bedford.

"My mother was a small woman who had fourteen children. I remember her coming out of the house to meet me. She said 'at least one of you got back'," he recalls. "My daddy was a big old rough farmer. The first time I had ever seen him cry was when I came home."

∼

Victory Plaza on the National D-Day Memorial is about an acre in size, semi-circular in shape, and ringed with flags of the thirteen Allied nations involved in the D-Day invasion.

The finished memorial will include a sprawling scene below the plaza that symbolizes the landing.

A sixteen-foot wall will represent the German bunkers that guarded the cliffs of Normandy. The realistic statue "Across the Beach" depicting of a GI pulling a wounded comrade will stand on the symbolic sands below the wall. A reflecting pool will symbolize the English Channel. A replica of a Higgins Landing Craft will symbolize the crossing of the Allied invaders.

Beneath the arch is another realistic statue, "The Final Salute," honoring those who fell in combat. The statue depicts an infantryman's rifle, with bayonet affixed, stuck into the ground. A combat helmet sits atop the rifle butt and and dog tags hang near the trigger.

The design of the education center near the memorial will recall the fortified bunkers that the soldiers encountered in Normandy. It will house four galleries, an auditorium and the 120-seat Arnold M. Spielberg Theater, named for the father of filmmaker Steven Spielberg. The elder Spielberg is a WWII veteran who fought in the Pacific.

Steven Spielberg, whose movie "Saving Private Ryan" renewed interest in D-Day, made a monetary contribution to build the education center but did not disclose the amount.

Richard Burrow, president of the D-Day Memorial Foundation, said that one of the galleries will feature rotating exhibits from the National D-Day Museum, which is opening on June 6 in New Orleans.

Before his death in February, "Peanuts" cartoonist Charles Schultz, a WWII veteran, led the fundraising campaign for the D-Day Memorial in Bedford. His widow, Jeannie Shultz, has taken over the duties.

Burrow said $8.7 million has been raised. The Commonwealth of Virginia will match the next $3.5 million in private contributions, he said, which will cover all construction costs and start the endowment to pay for operations.

~

Roy Stevens, eighty, and eighty-five-year-old Ray Nance, a Company A first lieutenant who was wounded on Omaha Beach, are the only two of Bedford's "D-Day boys" still living in the town.

Nowadays, Bedford is largely a bedroom community for folks who work in Roanoke or Lynchburg. It is still surrounded by scenic farms, including one where Elizabeth Teass lives. Lucille Boggess is a county supervisor. Green's Drug Store is closed. Ray Nance is a retired rural letter carrier. Roy Stevens is a retired rubber plant worker who lost a hand in an industrial accident.

Helen Stevens, who met and married Roy after the war, was working in a Bedford plant that made gas masks that summer when the telegrams arrived.

"One mother was working there when she heard that her son had been killed. She went home and never went back. Her husband later committed suicide," she said. "For a long time, Bedford was just like a funeral."

Justice on Trial

With the mind of a six-year-old child, Tommie Lee Hines ponders his predicament.

A twenty-year-old black man, he is charged with raping a white woman. She sits across a courtroom from him. Nearby are lawmen who say he confessed to the sexual assault at a railway depot in the nearby town of Decatur. But the people who know him best—his teachers and family—say he could not now remember the woman, the confession or even the attack, if indeed he committed it eight months earlier.

In the shade of a pecan tree outside the courthouse, a knot of Ku Klux Klansmen and their sympathizers speculate about "outside agitators" invading their town to support Hines. But understanding their racism is likely beyond the mind of the accused, who has an IQ of about thirty-nine.

Across the parking lot, Hines' supporters speak out with a defiance that friends say the defendant himself has never shown. "We ain't the same folk the klan scared twenty years ago," says a young woman. "They're dealing with a new black man and woman."

All around Tommy Lee Hines, a textbook case of Southern justice is being written. Old South and New South are clashing. But what is history to a man who can't remember the days of the week?

In the courtroom, the young man drops his gaze to the carpet, seemingly content to be ignored amid the legal and racial turmoil that will determine what happens to him for the rest of his life.

~

The trial comes down to whom to believe.

Decatur police detective Doyle Ward testifies that Hines, under gentle questioning, admitted committing three rapes. He says Hines took investigators to the scenes of the crimes and provided details. The confession is in the defendant's own words, the detective says.

The trial is for only one of the rapes. The victim says the attacker wore a plastic bag on his head like a bonnet—leaving his face uncovered. She positively points out Tommy Lee Hines as that man.

But his teachers and testers at a school for the retarded testify that Hines is incapable of relating the confession as written. The language is too sophisticated for him. Scared by authority figures and eager to please them, the young retarded man would likely admit to anything he thought the police wanted to hear.

If asked, "how many women did you rape, two or three," Hines would pick an answer just trying to be right, explained a defense witness.

School officials testify that a violent attack would be out of character for slow, subservient Tommy Lee Hines.

The trial is compared to the Scottsboro boys case of the 1930s. Eight black men were sentenced to death on doubtful charges of rape by two white women then. The trial took place in Decatur, Alabama.

Now, a hour's drive away, an all-white jury must decide another explosive rape case—and then face their neighbors with the verdict.

~

"He was seven before he ever talked," his daddy recalled. "But he was always a good boy. Always minded. Anything you'd tell him to do, he'd try to do it. He never sassed me or his mama. I never heard him say a cuss word."

Richard Hines doesn't believe his boy, Tommy Lee, is capable of committing a rape.

"You know, that boy has never been to a picture show in his life. He does watch TV some and try to color with crayons. But he don't know a nickel from a quarter.

"I always knew he was different from the rest of my children. I had nine boys and three girls, you know. But he ain't crazy, I'll tell you that. He's retarded, just different."

Neighbors say the Hines family has borne a heavy burden in recent years.

Tommy's mother is bedridden. Several years ago, David, one of his brothers, was found dead, shot in the back of the head. He was nineteen.

"He worked in a white-owned store and there was a rumor he was fooling around with the owner's daughter," said James Guster, a neighbor who drives Tommy to and from the trial.

"He's out on bond," a state trooper explained. "Has been since shortly after his arrest. We're liberal over here, son."

In Decatur, Tommy was a familiar figure but was rarely seen alone.

"Everybody knew Tommy," said Guster. "When we'd see him, he'd always be with relatives. We never saw him by himself."

"I never let him out to play much," said Richard Hines. "Bigger boys would try to hurt him. He got knocked down once trying to play football. I couldn't let him get hurt."

He didn't attend school as a boy but when the Cherry Street School—a center for the retarded—opened, he started going when in his early twenties.

Tommy was trainable and could perform some tasks, the center discovered, but he could never function in society on his own.

~

Most of Cullman County's 52,000 residents would just as soon have never heard of Tommy Lee Hines. A change of venue brought the trial, a civil rights protest march, an angry, awakened Klan, and an unwanted notoriety to the sleepy county seat of Cullman.

"Folks in Cullman County ain't mad at Hines," said a state trooper from Decatur assigned to guard the Cullman County courthouse.

"They're mad at that judge in Morgan County who sent his trial over here."

The arrest of the retarded black man sparked a summer of protests in Decatur.

The Southern Christian Leadership Conference organized marches and camp-ins.

The Rev. Richard B. Cottonreader came in as the SCLC project coordinator. Some white citizens denounced him as an "outside agitator."

"I got involved when some local people called the national office," he said. "I tried to arouse the community as best I know how."

He came and organized the black community and sought movement beyond this trial.

"Alabama's changing, but Decatur is more behind than the average town," he said. "Tommy Hines was the straw that broke the camel's back. I believe that Tommy Hines is a special person chosen by God to bear a cross for the black people of Decatur."

After Cottonreader and other protesters occupied the courthouse grounds in Decatur, the KKK retaliated.

"City officials wouldn't meet with us," said Bill McGlocklin, KKK Kleagle of north Alabama. "So we staged a counter-demonstration."

Robed Klansmen set up tents on the grounds and a tense confrontation ensued with black protesters marching around the KKK encampment.

"The grass was our's and the pavement theirs," said McGlocklin.

Neither group violated the other's turf. Often TV crews roamed between them.

But the court moved the trial down the road—from Decatur to Cullman.

Only about two percent of the Cullman populace is black. Most of those citizens live just outside of town in a place called "The Colony."

White folks say there was never any racial trouble here until the trial.

"We have our coloreds in The Colony down there," said a man in green work clothes and a red cap. "They're treated as good as any whites. They just stick to their business and we stick to ours. Their kids go to school with our's.

"The trouble is the outside niggers coming in and the news media."

~

In the courtroom, under oath, the victim identifies Tommy Lee Hines as her attacker. However, she admits that she was unable to pick his picture from five shown her before the trial and there was never a line-up of suspects.

Keith Russell, a Decatur policeman, testifies that Hines was acting suspiciously on a Decatur street and picked up. Riding in the squad car to the police station, lawmen said, Hines confessed to three rapes. Later, he signed a confession—*"ToMmy Ines."*

Tommy Lee Hines was found guilty of rape and sentenced to thirty years in prison. In March of 1980, the Alabama Court of Criminal Appeals overturned the conviction. He was granted bond and returned home for awhile. But on November 21, 1980, he was ruled incompent to stand trial and taken to Bryce Hospital, a mental health facility in Tuscaloosa.

Diamonds in the Rough

The aroma of frying onions is wafting out from the concession stand and the Eagles are singing "Take It Easy" over the PA system. Carrying the accordion he will use to play "Take Me Out to the Ball Game" during the seventh-inning stretch, retired FBI agent Sol Quinn sidles by a flower box of red geraniums to reach his seat behind home plate. Players from the New Market Rebels are raking and lining the infield.

Another evening of baseball bliss is set to commence in the Shenandoah Valley.

"I love it here," exclaims Julio Chinea, twenty-two, who grew up in Naples, Florida, and pitched for Miami Dade Junior College and Bluefield College in West Virginia to earn his spot on the Rebels. "Since I was in about the ninth grade, I'd heard about it (from older players) and I just always wanted to play in the Valley."

For the college players who have come for thirty-seven summers, the dusty diamonds of the Shenandoah Valley League are fields of dreams. They know that Mo Vaughn of the California Angels and Steve Finley of the Arizona Diamondbacks and scores of other major leaguers played here in summers past. They know that baseball "bird dogs" with radar guns and stopwatches sometimes sit amid the friendly fans behind the chicken-wire backstops.

"A lot of scouts come to games and the coaches have pretty good connections," explains Tom Perrin, twenty-one, a shortstop from West

Palm Beach, Florida, and the College of Charleston. "That's what you're here for."

They see the Valley as a step toward million dollar contracts and prime-time play. But even those who will never draw a baseball paycheck can gain from a summer spent living with a local family and working on a farm or corner grocery. Many experience an America that they knew only from TV.

"It's kinda like Mayberry here. Everybody knows everybody," marvels Charlie Wentzky, twenty, a pitcher from Anderson, South Carolina, and the College of Charleston. "It's amazing that there are people like this left in the world—with all the shootings and robberies and stuff. They don't lock their doors. Basically, they don't live by the watch. They come and go as they need to."

Players learn about social networks by watching the community unite to finance a season and welcome a team of strangers into its midst, explains Larry Strawderman, the Rebels' volunteer general manager.

"They learn life."

~

Two of the teachers are "Mama Jean" and "Big E."

New Market Rebels of several seasons ago gave the nicknames to Jean Morse, a wife, mother, hairdresser, school bus driver, cook and hostess, and her husband, Everett, a husky state trooper.

For the past five seasons, after every game, home and away, "Mama Jean" has fed the team. She cooks for twenty-five players—plus coaches and an occasional visiting parent or girlfriend—at her house with an inviting front porch located a few of blocks from Rebel Field. Afterward, players watch TV, play cards and talk for hours, often spending the night.

"My policy: I go to bed when I'm ready," said Jean Morse. "I woke up the other morning to find that nine players had slept over."

Scattered along Interstate-81, there are six teams in the Valley League: the Winchester Royals, Front Royal Cardinals, Harrisonburg Turks, Waynesboro Generals, Staunton Braves and the Rebels. With a population of 1,500, New Market is the smallest host community. It is a town without taverns or other late-night establishments.

"The team needs a place to group, bond, hang out and get to know each other," said Morse. "It's a home away from home."

The summer grocery bill is "astronomical," she admits.

"The food she puts out is amazing," said Chinea.

The menu after a recent Friday night home game included fried chicken, macaroni and cheese casserole and coleslaw. Sometimes there is pizza or spaghetti or lasagna or cold cuts for sandwiches.

"At two o'clock, I'm cleaning up the mess," said Morse, whose efforts are voluntary and self-financed.

There's one ironclad rule.

"If any have been drinking, they don't drive from the house. I take their car keys," she said. "And anybody who thinks college students don't drink beer is kidding themselves."

There is also the deterrent of "Big E," with his state patrol car parked in the driveway.

Not that there have ever been problems.

"The college coaches don't send bad boys up here," says Jay Zuspan, who has hosted players on his Christmas tree farm outside of New Market for six summers. "They won't send us trouble."

"You won't meet a more polite group of young men than these baseball players," echoes Morse, declining to name the only two exceptions in five seasons.

Some of the players keep in touch after they leave. Others don't. She follows all their careers.

"When Marshall McDougall from Florida State hit six home runs in one game this year, I said, 'Why, he slept on my couch'," she recalled. "I keep telling them, when they get to the big leagues, don't forget about Mama Jean in Virginia."

~

During the early innings, the setting sun warms the backs of the 400 or so fans who paid the $3 admission to Rebel Park. Massanutten Mountain looms above an outfield fence painted with advertisements from local merchants. Giggling teen-aged girls lean over the railing near the third base dugout to gaze at their favorite Rebels.

Charlie Wentzky is the cutest player, agree Kim Leitzel and Katelyn Linski, both 13. They come to most games, as do their contemporaries.

School is out, so "you get together at the game," explains Katelyn.

In the green chairs behind home plate sit the "grandstand managers," club members who pay $75 a year for this prime position for viewing, socializing and grousing at the umpire. Many are retirees from the nearby Bryce Mountain Resort. Visiting fans—mostly host families from other league towns—sit in bleachers near the first base dugout.

The Rebel Park announcer welcomes by name and hometown the visiting moms, dads, grandparents and girlfriends of players on both teams.

Between innings, some fans cut through a neighboring yard to get black raspberry sundaes or fresh peach shakes at Pack's Frozen Custard stand. Others spend $1.25 for a Rebel Park hot dog topped with those fried onions. Kids chase foul balls and return them for a pack of baseball cards.

"I enjoy watching the town turn out for games. The whole summer schedule is wrapped around this ball park," said Martha Sims. She and her husband, George, are both Lutheran ministers as well as family hosts for a player.

"This is baseball the way it was in the 1950s," says Mo Weber, the Rebels' 76-year-old batting coach.

Retired from coaching at the College of William and Mary, he banters easily with players who kid him about personally knowing Abner Doubleday or coaching Joe DiMaggio in Little League.

"The players are flat-out better today," he says. "They are physically bigger, stronger, faster, better conditioned. They know more about anatomy and physiology."

After seven decades or so of baseball, he loves to hear the ump say "batter up."

"I'm fortunate to still be in the game."

~

"You don't have time for much except baseball," says Carson Wiggins, twenty, a pitcher from Waynesboro, Georgia, and Georgia College in Milledgeville who is spending the summer with the Winchester Royals.

The league schedules forty games in fifty-five days. Then there are playoffs for the top teams. The longest road trip—between Staunton and Winchester—takes about ninety minutes by bus. The players are not paid, although the league picks up the tab for their airfare from home and back and helps to find them summer jobs.

On this night, Wiggins and the rest of the Royals are visiting Bing Crosby Field in Front Royal.

The crooner was grand marshal of the 1949 Apple Blossom Festival, explains Linda Keen, the Cardinals volunteer president. The next year, he hosted a movie premier in Front Royal and performed at a benefit and even donated his own money for the white cinder block stadium that now bears his name.

Wiggins is spending the summer about twenty miles away in Winchester, a bustling community known for its apple orchards and as the hometown of Patsy Cline.

"Winchester is big compared to Waynesboro," jokes Wiggins.

He is staying with the same family that hosted his brother, Daniel, two summers ago. Daniel just signed a contract with the Chicago Cubs organization.

Carson Wiggins is philosophical about his own future. If it includes a big league career, fine. For now, though, he is happy to spend his days working in Martin's Grocery and his nights playing baseball in the Valley.

Most of the players are hopeful of playing professionally, but they know the odds are long.

"My main goal since Little League—and the main goal of most of the players here—is just to keep playing as long as we can," said Jeff Reardon, a New Market Rebels pitcher from Siena College in Albany, New York.

"It's every kid's dream," said J. C. Bunch, a Front Royal Cardinals catcher from Austin, Texas, and Trinity College in San Antonio. "The league provides an opportunity to be seen by scouts."

So far, at least, they are enjoying the culture shock of living slow in the Valley.

"I don't think California has a town this small," says Tom Adinolfi, a New Market pitcher from San Jose State. "I'd been here two days and already people on the street were saying, 'Hi Tim'."

Dave Biery, who works at an auto parts dealership in Staunton, is president of the Valley League. The position pays $200 a year. Only coaches and umpires receive real salaries. Most everybody else is an unpaid volunteer. About twenty percent of the league budget comes from Major League Baseball through an NCAA program. The NCAA sanctions several such summer leagues scattered from Alaska to Cape Cod.

"Each team does its own recruiting. They compete with each other for players—as well as with other leagues," said Biery. "The main selling point is the quality of the league."

Since admissions pay the bulk of the bills, promotion is an important element of the league. There are contests for the best decorated lawn chairs, for instance. And New Market has an incongruous Chicken Man who cavorts during some games.

The team got a good deal on the suit through the Internet, explained GM Strawderman. "He's a Rebel chicken."

A Culture Marooned

On pleasant evenings, teenaged islanders congregate on the steps of the weathered post office and converse in a lilting parlance that traces to their Elizabethan forebears.

Ofttimes the talk is of leaving.

"There's more to do" on the mainland, explains Sandy Dise, fifteen, a tenth grader whose roots run generations deep in the scant island soil. "And you don't have to take a boat when you want to do it."

"We're losing the young people," laments Mayor Dewey Crockett, who is also assistant principal of the school, music director and organist at Swain Memorial United Methodist Church, and the undertaker. "With television and VCRs and the Internet, we're not as isolated as we once were."

Indeed, the remote island has changed more in recent decades than it did during several centuries following its discovery in 1608 by Captain John Smith, the leader of Jamestown.

Homes that didn't have phones until 1966 now have cable TV and computers. As its watermen suffer dwindling crab catches and tightening environmental regulation, the Tangier economy is turning toward tourism. But opportunity is still limited. The population has fallen from about 1,500 in 1900 to about 650 today.

A precious, marooned culture is endangered, many islanders fear.

"There's no other place like this," allows ninety-four-year-old Ruth Wallace Clark as she drives her golf cart down King Street. Her voice confirms the claim. Centuries of isolation have left a linguistic cadence and some pronunciations that are closer to Shakespearean English than to a Virginia drawl. "High tide," for example, sounds more like "hoy toyed" hereabouts. The beach on the northern end of the island is located "up'ards".

Tangier sits in the Chesapeake Bay, about eighteen miles from the western banks of Virginia and about twelve miles from Maryland's eastern shore. The island is about five miles long and less than two miles wide. Only a fourth of the 850 acres qualify as dry land. Its 250 or so houses are squeezed onto three ridges separated by marshes and tidal canals called "guts" and connected by several hump-backed bridges.

The streets are not much wider than sidewalks and most travel is by bicycle, electric golf cart, motor scooter or on foot. There are a few compact pick-up trucks for hauling stuff. As the dead and living vie for scarce space, tiny lawns are filling up with gravestones. The family names in the epitaphs are largely the same as those in the current phone directory: Crockett, Pruitt, Parks, Dise, Thomas, Wallace.

The first documented settlers were Joseph Crockett, his sons, and their wives and children. They came in 1778 to farm and to herd sheep and cattle. The founding families were fruitful, though, and there were few acres to cultivate. So islanders soon turned to the bounty of the bay—fish, oysters and crabs.

While the waters have long provided sustenance, Methodism has been the island's spiritual rock since Joshua Thomas converted during a trip to the mainland in 1805. The husband of one of Joseph Crockett's granddaughters, Thomas returned with enough fire and brimstone to ignite a religious movement that still guides practically every aspect of island life.

No alcoholic beverages or lottery tickets are sold on Tangier. In 1998, the town council rejected Hollywood offers to film "Message in a Bottle" on the island. The movie starred Paul Newman, Kevin Costner and Robin Penn Wright but the council read the script and rejected it because it featured scenes of sex and beer drinking.

On Sundays, worship begins with a frank and open "Class Meeting" in which the congregation shares personal and communal joys and concerns. Led by lay members, the tradition was begun by a denominational pioneer, John Wesley, but has long since been dropped by most Methodist churches. This hour-long session is followed by Sunday School, and by morning and evening services. There is another sermon and more hymns on Wednesday nights. Islanders wear T-shirts commemorating past revival meetings.

"We have strong family values, but this is not utopia," cautions Jean Crockett, the wife of the mayor, as well as one of the island's two nurses and an upper-grades English teacher. There are some illegal drugs, she said, and a couple of bootleggers who sell booze and beer.

But "it's a good place for kids to grow up," said Edward Landon, the island policeman, basketball coach and church youth director.

~

"Crabs are scarce. That's for sure. But it's not the watermen's doing," declares Kim Parks. "And we've been accused of raping the bay. That's plain and simple not the truth. We're just out to make a living."

Like his father and his father's father and his grandfather's father and now like his son, Parks is a Tangier waterman. He is up at 3:00 A.M. and out on the bay setting crab pots hours before dawn. Evenings find him at the shedding tanks in his crab shanty, which sits on pilings near the end of his dock. The island economy relies heavily on soft-shelled blue crabs—delicacies that can fetch $2 apiece, several times the price of the hard-shelled crustaceans.

As they mature, crabs shed their shells but quickly harden new ones. Crabs that are about to molt are called peelers—pronounced "pailers" on Tangier. Watermen catch peelers and keep them in tanks until they reach their soft-shelled stage. Then they are iced down and shipped live. Except on the Sabbath, the tasks are continuous.

"Being a waterman has always meant long hours, hard work and uncertain results," said the forty-four-year-old Parks.

Years ago, a thriving Chesapeake oyster industry was destroyed by shoreline run-off and other pollutants . Now environmental officials in Virginia and Maryland are concerned about a declining crab population. Strict catch limits are enforced and a huge no-crabbing zone has been established in a part of the bay near Tangier. There is a freeze on issuing crabbing licences.

At the same time, increases in imported crab meat from Asia keep prices down for the watermen.

"About ninety-five percent of our living comes from the water," said Mayor Crockett. So the island economy is being squeezed.

To compensate, wives and daughters of watermen are cultivating tourism. From April through October, two cruise ships dock daily. The "Chesapeake Breeze" makes a one and a half hour trip from Buzzards Point, near Reedville, Virginia. The "Steven Thomas" takes forty-five minutes to reach the island from Crisfield, Md. About 25,000 people visited last year—mostly on day trips.

Local folk have opened several seafood restaurants, a couple of gift shops and three bed and breakfasts. After living on the mainland, Wallace and Shirley Pruitt returned to open Shirley's Bayview Inn on West Ridge in a house built by his maternal grandfather in 1905.

"My mother spent her whole life here and I was born in this house," said Pruitt, sixty. When his siblings moved away, he couldn't bear selling it. "This house brought me back. I couldn't see somebody outside the family living here."

Business has been so brisk that he has built guest cottages in the back yard.

As tourists wander the narrow streets, they see wooden boxes nailed to power poles and containing recipes for crab cakes, corn pudding and other island specialities. They can drop in a quarter and take one home.

When the cruise boats dock, the visitors are greeted by several women who conduct fifteen-minute tours in golf carts. Charging $3 per rider, Gina Crockett said she gets twenty or so customers per day in the summer.

The wife of a waterman, Crockett, thirty-five, said she loved growing up on Tangier and visits the mainland only once or so a month. She believes that the close-knit community, where every neighbor keeps a caring and attentive eye on every child, is a blessed place to rear her three offspring.

But she doubts that her children will stay as she has.

"They'll probably want to go to college," said Gina Crockett.

∿

In recent years, enrollment has ranged from about 100 to 110 at the Combined School, which goes from kindergarten through twelfth grade. There were nine graduates in June, recalled Jean Crockett, 50, the English teacher. Three are going to college. Three joined the navy. Two girls stayed to marry islanders. One boy "went on the water" with his father.

Most of those who leave for college won't return. "This is not an easy place to make a living," said Jean Crockett.

Justin Landon, the sixteen-year-old son of the island policeman, figures he will join the air force after graduating from the Combined School in two years.

Like other teens, he likes the island but admits to occasional boredom. For fun, they swim off the docks and at the beach; go fishing, crabbing and cruising in small skiffs with outboard motors; play video games, watch TV and videotaped movies; and play basketball. And they drive around and around the island on motor scooters or in golf carts.

"That's about it," said Justin Landon.

Increasingly, island families keep a car on the mainland for activities there. For better or worse, horizons are broadening.

"They're still sheltered growing up here," said Edward Landon. "So it's a shock" for the kids "when they leave at eighteen for the mainland."

He knows from experience. After military service and living off the island for several years, he returned to raise his family. There's not as much for teenagers to do here, he says, "and that's a good thing."

There are a couple of small groceries on Main Ridge and an air strip for small planes. A doctor and dentist make regular visits. Except when the bay freezes over, a mail boat comes every day—taking passengers at $12 apiece for a round-trip to the Maryland shore. So a family trip to the mainland can be an expensive outing.

There is a rhythm to island life. The crab boats leave in pre-dawn darkness and return in late afternoon. The cruise boats arrive in late morning and tourists abound for a few hours and then the boats depart and the populace returns to normal levels and activities. The mail boat docks at 1:15 P.M. and the post office closes while the mail is sorted. At 2:30 P.M., much of the town is gathered and chatting when the post office reopens and mail is picked up. Then folks ride off on their bikes and golf carts. Teenagers gather in the evenings and the policeman makes his rounds.

Crime are rare. Indeed, islanders can recall only four homicides in over two centuries. The most recent was the result of an altercation between two watermen in the 1960s.

But now the population temporarily swells daily with outsiders bringing notions as well as needed dollars. A new visitors' center is in the works, said Mayor Crockett. "But we don't want to get too commercial."

In many ways, islanders would like to keep things the way they always have been.

An Ear to the Sky

The world's largest landlocked machine seems a tad out of place in the rugged isolation of Deer Creek Valley.

But this patch of scarce flatland, sparsely populated and surrounded by Allegheny Mountains, is the ideal home for the gigantic, gleaming white contraption that looms above the neighboring farms.

For four decades, a remote Pocahontas County hamlet has been "the center of American radio astronomy," explained Mark McKinnon, associate scientist and deputy site director of the National Radio Astronomy Observatory facility at Green Bank.

Shielded by the mountains from earthly interference such as radio stations, Green Bank's sensitive telescopes have explored distant galaxies by collecting radio waves since 1958. Now construction crews are nearing completion of a colossal new high-tech radio telescope that could enable astronomers to examine uncharted reaches of the universe and perhaps alter our conceptions of time and space and creation.

The new Green Bank Telescope or GBT will be "the largest dynamic structure on Earth," said McKinnon. Earthlings' only bigger machines are aircraft carriers and similarly sized ocean vessels.

The project has taken more than a decade. It began shortly after the collapse of Green Bank's twenty-six-year-old radio telescope in late 1988. Senator Robert Byrd (D-W. Va.), famous for looking after the home-folks, quickly convinced Congress to appropriate $75 million to begin building a much bigger replacement. After considerable complications and delay, the new GBT—weighing 16 million pounds and standing as tall as the Washington Monument—is expected to be completed this summer.

Having watched the telescope rise like a monstrous roller-coaster, its neighbors are curious about what it will find and thankful for the dollars that its construction brought into a hard-up, hardscrabble community.

The region was initially chosen for an observatory because of "its lack of potential for economic development," said McKinnon.

Pocahontas County is about one hundred miles long and fifty miles wide, but only about 8,000 people live there. On the winding mountain roads, some school buses take two hours to reach the high school in Marlinton, the county seat. The Monogahela National Forest covers much of the area. Steady paychecks are hard to come by. The observatory employs 110 people. Other residents are farmers or loggers. There is mostly seasonal work at Snowshoe Ski Resort on the far side of Little Mountain.

"You have to string together several jobs to make a living," said Tony Samons, the Green Bank barber, a finish carpenter and the preacher for a congregation of about forty souls at the Church of God.

"There are three sets of people here," allowed Samons, who charges $4 for a haircut. "First there are the natives. To be a native, your grandpa had to be born here."

Samons, who was born in Kentucky and moved here in 1979, puts himself and many of the observatory people in the second group of long-time residents who have reared families hereabouts, are acquainted with everybody, "but aren't natives."

The third group are the "real outsiders"—transient construction workers or visiting hunters, he said. "The natives call them pilgrims."

It's a stubbornly insular place, where folks mind their own business.

"There are still a few people around who would sell you moonshine if you wanted it," said Samons. "But more grow marijuana. They plant it in the national forest or between rows in cornfields."

On Sundays, Green Bank's church-goers have a choice of the Liberty Presbyterian, Wesley Chapel United Methodist, Hebron Baptist or the aforementioned Church of God. Wares at the Green Bank General Store range from handsewn quilts to crossbows. A homemade ice cream sandwich costs 69¢, a double-edged ax goes for $45 and a used mandolin will set you back $145. For a fee, the Mountain State Meat Market will turn a hunter's venison into sausage, jerky or cured deer ham.

Green Bank has a clinic, a public library, an elementary school, a post office, a hardware store, a volunteer fire department and rescue squad, a bank, an Oldsmobile dealer, an antique store, a one-chair barber shop and a combination convenience store, gas station and pizza parlor.

And now it has a new, world-class GBT—which stands for "Great Big Telescope," according to local humorists.

~

The Green Bank Telescope has been described as an ear to the sky. But that's not exactly right.

A radio telescope doesn't "hear" radio signals from outer space any more than a car radio "hears" a Dixie Chicks song that is broadcast by a country music station. "Both have an antenna that collects radio waves," said McKinnon. The car radio converts these waves into sounds. The radio telescope translates them into images or graphs that enable astronomers to learn about unseen objects in the distant universe.

Radio signals reaching Earth from faraway galaxies are feeble—often barely discernible. So astronomers are constructing ever-bigger antennae to catch them.

"Just like you can capture more raindrops in a bigger bucket," explained McKinnon. "The GBT has two acres of collecting area. You could build eight houses on it. It will be the largest, fully steerable radio telescope in the world."

In addition to its size, though, the GBT has new technologies aimed at helping astronomers examine the edges of the universe.

"First, there's the offset feed arm," said McKinnon. In all radio telescopes, the antenna is a parabolic dish that catches the radio signal and focuses it into a receiver. Earlier models used support arms to hold the receiver over the middle of the dish. However, these support arms blocked some of the incoming radio waves. The GBT's offset feed arm holds the receiver without interfering with incoming signals. The same design is used on some small home TV satellite dishes.

Another technological advance is the GBT's "active surface," said McKinnon. The surface of its parabolic dish is a mosaic of 2,004 movable aluminum panels mounted on "actuators." As the giant dish is turned and tilted to face the incoming radio waves, computers adjust the actuators to insure that the surface is absolutely smooth and is focusing the desired signal at the receiver.

The telescope is surrounded by twelve ground range finders that use lasers to scan the surface of the dish for any irregularities caused by sun or wind. If a hot summer sun has expanded an exposed section of the frame by a fraction of an inch, for instance, the lasers will trigger a corrective movement of the surface panels.

The collected radio signals from space are transmitted via fiber optics from the telescope receiver to a control room and observatory about a mile away. To keep its electronic equipment from tainting the signal from space with their own faint radio waves, this control room is lined with copper wallpaper.

Astronomers use old diesel cars and trucks to drive to and from the telescope—eliminating the interference generated by spark plugs in conventional gas-powered vehicles.

The 16 million pound telescope sits on sixteen gigantic steel wheels that roll on a circular metal track with a diameter of 210 feet. The track rests on a reinforced concrete foundation that extends twenty-five feet below ground to the bedrock.

A gigantic gear raises and lowers the elevation of the huge, but delicately balanced, parabolic dish and the offset arm that angles over it. This whole asymmetrical shebang is made of welded steel beams—which had to be trucked in over the mountainous roads.

"Despite its enormity, the GBT is designed to operate more precisely than a quartz watch," said McKinnon.

~

Astronomers from around the world will use the GBT.

The National Radio Astronomy Observatory is a facility of the National Science Foundation, a federal agency, and operated under an agreement with Associated Universities Incorporated, a consortium of academic institutions. The National Radio Astronomy Observatory has other telescopes at Socorro, New Mexico, and Kitt Peak, Arizona.

The facilities operate under an "open sky policy," explained McKinnon. Leading astronomers submit research proposals and requests for time on a telescope. A panel of scientific referees decide which projects are worthy. Highly trained telescope operators help conduct these searches of outer space. Sometimes the data is transmitted over the Internet, sparing astronomers the trip to isolated telescope sites.

There are trade-offs for scientists and families living here in the center of the National Radio Quiet Zone, set up by the Federal Communications Commission to protect the purity of signals from outer space. There's no better place for a radio telescope. But it's an hour-and-a-half drive to the grocery store or a movie. Winter weather can be brutal. On the other hand, by staying on the second grade honor roll, eight-year-old Caitlin McKinnon earns free skiing privileges for herself and her parents on the the nearby Snowshoe slopes.

Acceptance into the community is sometimes slow. Fertile flatland is scant and some farmers resented that the observatory took over such a prime spot. West Virginia has been stung by companies that deserted the state after clearing forests for timber or bulldozing mountain tops for coal.

There are lingering suspicions that "outsiders come to take," said McKinnon, who has lived at Green Bank for eight years.

"The mountains are beautiful but harsh," said Samons, the barber and preacher. "I wouldn't live anywhere else."

～

The Green Bank telescope is finished and exploring the universe.

Death and Life in the Coalfields

They laid the earthly remains of Jesse Jones to rest Sunday in a polished pine box shoveled beneath the rocky soil of Appalachia.

"Jesse was and is a coal-mining man," said the Rev. Donald Butcher. "Jesse's grandpa on his daddy's side died in a mine explosion."

Then, as the preacher comforted Jesse's widowed mother, Lulu Belle Jones, somebody turned on a CD of Vince Gill singing.

"Go rest high on that mountain. Son, your work on Earth is done," the haunting, disembodied voice rang out. *"Go to heaven a-shouting love for the Father and the Son."*

There wasn't a dry eye in the crowded chapel of the Tomblyn-Whitescarver Funeral Home, located about ten miles from the Sago coal mine where Jesse Jones and eleven of his trapped co-workers perished last week after a mine shaft collapsed.

"God has twelve new angels," said the sign at the Go-Mart in Buckhannon. At the entrance to the Sago mine itself, twelve big, black bows were tied to a chain-link fence.

Preacher Butcher read the lyrics from a song titled "A Coal-Mining Man."

"Daylight or dark, rain or shine," the words went. *"It don't matter much, down in the mine."*

As the world watched the sad saga of the helpless men who died in the mine in Upshur County, thousands of their fellow miners quietly continued their own dusty work in the black seams deep below the hills and hollows.

"Coal mining runs deep in the blood of many of our families," said Rev. Butcher. "Coal miners are a different breed."

His daddy was a coal miner who warned that the job was dangerous, dark and dirty, said Ron Varner.

But four decades ago, he didn't heed the old man's advice not to work under the mountain, and twelve neighboring deaths would not deter him on another raw winter afternoon.

"Buddy, I'm two years from retirement. I can't bail now," said Varner, fifty-eight, as he headed into the evening shift at the Eastern Associated Coal Corporation Federal No. 2 Mine beside a gurgling creek known as Miracle Run.

"You've never seen dark like you see in a coal mine," said Mike Caputo, a United Mine Workers of America official who spent twenty years working underground. Some mined coal seams are only twenty-eight inches high, he said, "so you have to do everything laying down."

Every day, as miners ride the "man trip" on rails that extend miles into the shafts, they know the cart might not bring them out alive. And hazards linger even into retirement, said Caputo.

"About 1,500 former miners die of black lung disease every year" from careers of breathing coal dust, he said.

The reasons that miners give for risking their lives and health in what many outlanders view as an occupational hell can be summed up in a word: Money.

"It's as good a paying job as you'll find around in this area," said Ted Johnson, forty, who followed his father into the mines right after graduating from high school at the age of eighteen.

The Census Bureau puts the median household income in West Virginia at about $30,000, well below the national median of about $42,000. The West Virginia Coal Association said the average annual wage for a miner in the state is about $54,000 a year. With overtime, most union miners make from $60,000 to $70,000 a year in these boom times for coal production, said Caputo.

Why folks in West Virginia become miners "is not a difficult question to answer," the UMWA political organizer allowed.

"We have families to raise. We work so our kids can go to college like the mine owners' children do," said Caputo. "Most miners don't want their children in the mines, even though a lot of them do end up working there."

When coal prices fall, though, mines close and miners lose these paychecks, at least temporarily.

"I've been laid off twice—for two years both times," said Mark Dorsey, who has been a coal miner for thirty-two of his fifty years. But since 1995, he has been working steadily on a 4:00 P.M. to midnight shift as a "timber man," installing wooden posts to bolster sagging roofs of mine shafts.

"In this area, if you can get full medical coverage and a decent wage, that's a good job," he said. "You can take care of your family."

In mountain communities of this hardscrabble state, where coal and labor are as abundant as comfort and opportunity are scarce, life has been much the same for generations of miners.

"My dad was one, and I wanted to be like my dad. That's the truth," said Eddie Hawkins, forty-five. "I've been laid off a couple of times but it's made a good living for me."

The proximity of the deaths in the non-union Sago mine about sixty miles to the south hit him hard, he conceded. "It bothered me a lot. I asked my wife and my little girl to pray for me. It was close to home."

But he has no plans to pull out and look for a safe job in the sunshine.

"God watches over me in there," he said.

Mines are located where the coal seams are easiest to exploit, often in hard-to-reach locales. So more than a century ago, mine companies built communities for workers and their families. They created company houses to live in and company stores to shop in, and even printed company scrip to use as a local currency.

From Mingo County to the Cheat River, children in mining communities grew up seeing their fathers with faces black with coal dust. They performed in school skits about Mother Jones organizing a miners union. The West Virginia state seal even depicts a miner holding a pickax.

The miners own their homes now, many of them small houses perched on scant patches of flat earth. They shop at Wal-Mart and drive their pickups an hour on winding mountain roads to reach their jobs.

They are reluctant to abandon the lore of their forebears or the deep kinship they feel for the rugged outdoors, expressed in a love of hunting and fishing.

"This is home," explained Varner. "It's hard to move away from home."

Unwilling to move, folks turn to jobs in the industry spawned by their region's most abundant natural resource: coal. The National Mining Association said about 24,000 people are employed in the West Virginia coal industry.

Every veteran of years spent "under the hill" has a tale of narrow escape.

Dorsey's closest call came during a roof collapse. As the timber man, he was working several feet behind a "continuous miner" when the new opening collapsed atop the machine. Its operator was protected by a canopy, and co-workers pulled him from beneath the rocks.

As the shaft filled with choking, blinding, explosive coal dust, "that was the most scared I ever was," said Dorsey. "At first, we were afraid to move, because it might cause another collapse."

Unable to see, "we did a lot of hollering to make sure each other was all right," he said. Then they carefully backed out of the shaft.

Conditions inside the mines have improved over the decades. Most shafts now are high enough for workers to stand upright, although the height is still determined by the size of the coal seam. The continuous miners are outfitted with water sprays that tamp down the coal dust.

There is even a "dinner hole"—a chamber with a picnic table—where miners eat, said Bill Deegan, fifty-six, who works underground as an electrician and mechanic.

But the job sites are still harsh. Miners gear up for their shifts of eight to 10 hours at a bath house, and clean up there afterward.

"You change into several layers of clothes," said Dorsey. "It gets mighty cold down there."

In the scores of tiny towns with signs saying "Pray For Our Miners' Families" in front of the Dairy Queens and used car lots, the coal culture is unlikely to change soon.

The West Virginia Coal Association says recoverable coal reserves are found in forty-three of the state's fifty-five counties. As long as there are profits for the coal companies and paychecks for the miners, the dangers will continue.

"You don't know if you're coming out every day," Dorsey explained. "But if you dwell on it, you can't be a coal miner."

Now, once again, this harsh land was reclaiming its children.

In nearby Philippi, Jackie Weaver, fifty-two, was buried on a snowy hillside beside the grave of his son, Jackie Jr., who died in 1982 at the age of eleven in a moped accident. Among the items in the elder Weaver's casket were a camouflage hunting cap, a homemade "Happy Birthday Daddy" card made of yellow construction paper, and a child's drawings of a father in a miner's hard hat.

Weaver, who spent twenty-six years working in the mines, always wrote "Jesus saves" in the coal dust of the cart that took him and other miners into the dark shaft, recalled his cousin, Scotty Felton.

In the casket of Jesse Jones, forty-four, were pictures of his daughters, Sarah and Katelyn, and an embroidered pillow reading "Daddy's Girl."

Butcher spoke movingly of the hard times that folks in these parts have endured for generations.

"My family were coal miners," he recalled. "When my grandpa was twenty-six or twenty-seven, he was setting a charge in a coal mine and the explosion blinded him. He never set eyes on me, and he walked with a cane for the rest of his life."

But the preacher said he loved and missed his "paw-paw," whose disability entitlement from the mining company came to $18 a month.

Speaking of Jones, he said, "Here's a young man, just forty-four years old, who spent twenty-one years, nearly half his life, in a coal mine. God gives us people who are heroes and we don't even realize it."

~

A MOONPIE MURDER
AND OTHER MAYHEM

~

The Algiers Point Militia   *Photo by Rick McKay*

Murder in a Mill Town

Now it comes down to the story of two young women, one in a grave in Tennessee, the other accused of putting her there.

They grew up in small Southern towns at about the same time, but their lives could not have been more different. They knew each other for only a short, tragic time. Now one is dead, mourned by family and friends. The other is on trial for her life, friendless and despised—as she has been most of her life.

It is a brutal story, a stark saga of good and bad that has hung for nearly a year over this north Georgia carpet mill town, permeating the air like the mist from the Great Smoky Mountains.

It has taken several days to seat a jury in the Whitfield County Courthouse. It's hard to find people who don't already have deep feelings about the case.

~

Life has never been easy for Janice Buttrum.

Her mother gave her away, shortly after her birth, to people willing to pay the hospital bill. She never knew who her real father was.

On trial for murder, her life story comes out in a competency hearing.

Born in neighboring Bartow County, Janice was raised by R. V. and Elizabeth Adcock in a three-room wooden house with no indoor plumbing.

The Adcocks never formally adopted the baby girl, although she would later take their last name. A funeral director in Adairsville made the arrangement in which the infant was exchanged for payment for her delivery and her mother's hospital stay.

Marie Beavers, her biological mother, had made the same deal for previous births, according to testimony. The Adcocks, then a middle-aged couple, had lost a premature baby shortly before Janice was born.

The Adcocks drank heavily, according to court documents. Social workers and a visiting nurse who had known Janice since she was five years old said the little girl was reared in filth and neglect.

Carol Rose, a public health nurse who visited the household to treat Mrs. Adcock for psoriasis, said the foster mother would hit the child with a switch without provocation and curse her.

"She threw her real mother up to her. She'd tell her what a bad reputation her mother had and tell her Janice was going to end up just like her," Mrs. Rose testified.

In the courtroom, Janice's former grammar school teachers recalled her as a "loner" who was ridiculed because of her ragged clothes.

"The children always made fun of her, always ran up to her and would run back from her because of her body odor and her appearance. She would not try to fight the other children. She just tried to ignore them, I guess," testified Mary Caruthers, who taught Janice in the fourth grade at Adairsville Elementary School.

"Her hair was very matted. Her face, her body was always filthy. Her clothes were filthy," the teacher recalled.

Elizabeth Adcock would take Janice to the city dump to scavenge for clothes, according to the testimony, and other children would see her there and tease her.

When she was twelve, Janice's life became even worse. R. V. Adcock, her foster father, died. Her foster mother moved out of the little house and into an even smaller travel trailer, living with another man, according to the testimony.

Carol Rose, the public health nurse, said it was about this time that she heard Mrs. Adcock tell Janice: "This is not your house. I can make you leave at any time."

Janice was often absent from school. It was through this truancy that she became acquainted with Marvin Dickerson, a social worker for the school system. While visiting the trailer to check on Janice, he heard the foster mother describe how she had "bought Janice. That she had paid the hospital bill and owned her."

In court on truancy charges, Dickerson said, Janice was told by the woman who had raised her "I hate you and I never want to see you again."

Afterward, Janice was put into a series of state institutions and foster homes, rarely staying any place longer than a few months. She ran away often.

"Janice was probably the most neglected child I've ever seen in my life," said Dickerson. He said she once spent the night with two twenty-seven-year-old men "simply because they promised her a little love and affection."

She was barely fourteen years old at the time, he recalled.

When she was fifteen, Janice Adcock married Danny Buttrum.

A short, wiry man with sunken cheeks, he was 10 years older than Janice. He had a history of drug and alcohol abuse and was wanted by the law. Months earlier, Danny had escaped from a Cobb County work camp where he was serving time for repeated convictions for driving under the influence.

Heavy-set, with frizzy brown hair usually pulled back into a pony-tail, Janice already looked older than her years. By August of 1980, when Janice was nineteen, the Buttrums had a nineteen-month-old daughter named Marlene. Janice was pregnant again. They lived in Dalton, where Danny was working as a tire repairman at a truck stop.

~

Early in the summer of 1980, Demetra Parker drove to Dalton in the two-tone tan, 1975 Buick Riviera that her daddy had given her a year before as a high school graduation present. She was also nineteen that summer, a pretty, dark-haired young woman who had grown up in Kenton, a farming community in western Tennessee.

Demetra was kind of quiet and shy and modest, said Kenny Parker, a brother who was two years older. She sang in the choir of the First Baptist Church in Kenton, he said, "but she didn't think she could sing good. She must not have been able to hear herself because she could really sing."

She came from a close-knit family. After finishing school, she lived awhile with an older sister in Tennessee before determining that she was ready to leave the comfortable nest of kinship. She moved to Dalton, a hard-working community on the edge of Appalachia, to be near a boyfriend who had earlier made this migration.

Demetra Parker got a job on the midnight-to-eight shift of a carpet bindery plant and began setting up a new life. But she remained close to her family.

"She called home a couple of times every week," said Kenny. "We were always tight. You know how boys are with their little sisters.

"She came from a big family in a small country town where everybody knows everybody. She was well loved."

Late that summer, Demetra was living in the Country Boy Inn, just south of Dalton and right off Interstate-75 on Carbondale Road. Her rent—$50 a week—was steep for a young woman just starting out on her own and she was scheduled to move into a house with a girlfriend on September 3.

When she didn't check out or answer phone calls that morning, the motel owner went to check on Demetra.

He found her dead on the floor.

~

Danny and Janice Buttrum were also living at the Country Boy Inn at the time.

Demetra would coo to their child.

"She was crazy about little babies," said Kenny. His sister was the motherly type, always advising girlfriends who had problems with their boyfriends.

Now, hardened police were taken aback at the grisly crime scene. Demetra Parker had been stabbed scores of times, strangled with a coat hanger, sexually assaulted with an electric toothbrush.

On the same day the body was found, the Buttrums were arrested in Pensacola, Florida. Danny and the baby were sitting in Demetra Parker's car. Janice was picked up in a nearby store, buying food.

~

The Buttrums were tried separately. In Danny's trial, witnesses said that he had told them how he and Janice killed Demetra Parker while their little daughter crawled around and played nearby. After a long evening of drinking beer, they had knocked on their neighbor's door and jumped her when she opened it. She was stabbed repeatedly with a knife with a short blade and raped while she was still alive and bleeding.

Testifying for the defense, Danny Buttrum's mother said he had been dropped on his head as a baby and was never the same afterward. No matter. It took the jury less than an hour to find him guilty of murder, rape and car theft.

Janice Buttrum was also convicted of murder.

Both were sentenced to be executed. Neither was. Danny Buttrum hung himself to death in his jail cell. After giving birth to her second child while waiting on death row, Janice Buttrum's sentence was changed to life.

Around her hometown in Tennessee, so many people turned out to mourn Demetra Parker that they held two funerals.

The Big "O" Around the "Big A"

Beltways—like zippers and instant coffee—came into vogue in the hurry-up decades following World War II as an ambitious America rushed to make up for lost years. A nation too busy for buttons and too preoccupied for percolation certainly couldn't slow down for city traffic congestion. So right from the start, beltways were a planned part of the massive interstate highway network that would zip a high-octane post-war populace hither and yon on six-lane concrete corridors.

When Congress passed the Federal-Aid Highway Act in 1944 creating the interstate highway system, the lawmakers declared that 2,300 of the 40,000 miles of expressways to be built would be "limited-access urban circumferential routes." These would provide wide paths around cities and let travelers dodge local traffic.

There would be metropolis-to-metropolis superhighways. And there would be city-encircling bypasses to keep interior streets unjammed. Beltways would let cars bound for elsewhere go around—rather than passing through—the downtowns and stoplights and rush hours.

Under the federal law, dozens of cities got beltways—Baltimore and Buffalo, Cincinnati and Columbus, Minneapolis, Washington and Wichita. These and many other cities were looped, or in some cases half-mooned, by bypasses as the interstate highway system crisscrossed the country.

Atlanta, the bold new city of the South, naturally got a beltway. Interstate-285, a sixty-four-mile, multi-lane expressway, was completed in 1969 and became a big concrete "O" around the South's "Big A."

Dubbed "The Perimeter," it was routed an average of nine miles from downtown Atlanta. The longest sections of I-285 run through the suburbs of Fulton and DeKalb counties. Other stretches are located in Cobb and Clayton counties. About twenty percent of The Perimeter is within the western boundary of the city of Atlanta.

"The original purpose was to provide a bypass route around the city so traffic that came in on the interstates would not have to go through to get to the other side," recalled Howell Reeves, deputy commissioner of the Georgia Department of Transportation.

But as America's beltways were built and buckled, a curious and unexpected phenomenon occurred. The cities that the beltways surrounded would leap out to them. Development sprang up alongside the perimeter highways, skipping over undeveloped terrain to reach them. Stores deserted downtowns and relocated beside the beltways. Shopping centers popped up at the interchanges. Suburban communities were built just beyond the band of commerce that hugged the circular highways. Jobs moved out from the central city, too, and property values surged.

In city after city, beltways became rings of prosperity and activity. In extreme cases, where the shuffle from downtown became a stampede, a city could become an economic doughnut. In other situations, urban growth was just dispersed.

Oops, the federal planners noted, unanticipated consequences.

As roads that went nowhere and never ended, the beltways passed by everything and could be departed only occasionally and predictably at established exits. Retailers found them irresistible. Hotels discovered a steady stream of customers. Airports and sports stadiums were built by the beltways. As suburbs and apartment complexes sprang up around the beltways, businesses found a pink-collar army of skilled, reliable and relatively undemanding housewives and single women who would first operate typewriters and later computer terminals.

A beltway often became a border. Citizens of a prosperous periphery population rarely ventured inside. Jobs, entertainment, schools, hospitals, amusement, housing, restaurants, sports, shopping—anything they wanted could be found alongside the circle of concrete.

Instead of being mainly bypasses for travelers headed beyond, many of America's bustling beltways became orbital Main Streets.

The Perimeter around Atlanta both fit and defied the pattern.

Since I-75 and I-85 both ran through the city before The Perimeter was built, some traffic still came downtown, like it or not.

"Atlanta built the in-town connector first. The development boom in the 1960s in partly attributable to that," said Tony Dowd, developer of preconstruction for the Georgia Department of Transportation. "Some cities built their bypass systems first around the cities, and the growth and development moved out to the perimeter and never came back."

Some of that happened in Atlanta, too, as generations of drivers know.

Since completion of The Perimeter, growth around the city has far outpaced that of the central districts. Employment in the downtown business district dwindled while jobs abounded around The Perimeter.

"Employment has not risen as the changing Atlanta skyline suggests," the federal government said in a report on the effects of beltways. "In this context, the attractiveness of beltway locations to office users appears to have harmed downtown Atlanta."

It wasn't just jobs. People also moved out to The Perimeter.

"The Atlanta beltway had significant effects on real estate investments in the region," said the federal report. "Developers of multi-family housing, suburban office parks and towers and shopping centers have all sought sites visible and/or accessible from I-285."

Greenbriar Mall. Cumberland Mall. The Galleria. Perimeter Mall. Perimeter Place. Northlake Mall. All are adjacent to I-285.

To some, The Perimeter became Atlanta's noose. To all, the "Big O" helped shape the destiny of the South's "Big A."

That giant circular traffic jam that drivers curse in Southern drawls has changed Atlanta's culture, economy and history.

Who knew?

Football and Fraternity

I dragged my family to this leafy, gothic campus to watch my beloved Florida State Seminoles roll over the Duke Blue Devils. Exploring the grounds the next day, we happened upon the Sigma Alpha Epsilon section and I thought back to that glorious Southern symbiosis of football and fraternity.

The long-haired, bellbottomed Sixties had not yet arrived in Tallahassee, Florida, in the autumn of 1964 when I pledged SAE. Football was sacred and fraternity boys dressed accordingly for Saturday worship at Doak Campbell Stadium. We wore navy blue blazers, cuffed khakis, oxblood Weejuns, no socks, striped ties and buttoned-down Gant shirts - white, because sweat stains show too starkly on light blue oxford cloth. The fashion mavericks wore black-and-white saddle shoes, called rah-rahs.

This dress code has been eased a bit in subsequent decades.

"Nobody wears coats and ties. It's too hot," said Temp Phillips, a Nineties era SAE at the University of Georgia. "Most people wear khaki pants and polo-type shirts."

There are other changes, of course. There are more African-American fraternity brothers, for instance, and hell week has been banned. Few fraternities now have a "house mother"—required by colleges in my era to maintain a semblance of sobriety and civilization.

But the basic rituals of a football weekend have remained for generations of fraternity brothers at Ole Miss and UNC and Grambling and other Southern campuses.

Dates are mandatory. This requirement is an occasional source of desperation. "I know a guy who paid someone $10 to get him a date," said Greg Belletti, an SAE at Georgia Tech.

Usually, though, somebody's girlfriend is willing to "fix up" the socially impaired brethren with a sorority sister. On one such occasion, between the arrangement and my arrival, a young lady with whom I was to share a Saturday actually forgot my name, remembering only that it sounded like Pop Tart.

In a situation fraught with potential for humiliation, these coupled strangers spend ten or so hours together. The activities often begin with a pre-game lawn party.

At Florida State, the SAE house is next door to the Kappa Alpha house, and the fraternities held simultaneous festivities. For some reason forgotten in the fog of time, both groups thought it would impress female guests to chant louder than the neighbors.

Drinks raised, we would shout, "Hotty toddy, Gawd a'mighty. Who the hell are we? Bim bam, by damn. We're the SAE."

Thereafter, the KAs would holler back, "Wheat, barley, alfalfa. Give 'em hell Kappa Alpha. Wheat, barley, hay. Give 'em hell KA."

These scholarly exchanges would continue until everyone headed to the stadium. On those hallowed grounds, precious memories were made—or sometimes forgotten in the fourth quarter haze of bourbon and Cokes in soggy paper cups.

Love of football and alma mater is in-bred for a sort of Southern boy who learns to say "Roll Tide" or "Go You Hairy Dawgs" only shortly after he is taught to address his elders as "ma'am" or "sir." Often they have followed fathers and friends to Knoxville or Chapel Hill or other such sanctuaries. Their priorities seem skewed to outsiders, but they are secure in this heritage.

Their shared elation when, say, the FSU Seminoles beat the Florida Gators is hard for the uninitiated to fathom. But for these sons of the South, there are few more joyous days in life.

Losses, however, rarely ruined a post-game party.

By then, blazers were gone, ties were loose, and, after five hours or so together, the coupling had either proved successful or not. Pairings hardly mattered, though, because everybody squeezed into a sweaty mass that pulsated in front of a band that played "Louie, Louie" at least once a set.

Mine was the era of soul music—called beach music in the Carolinas—and I cannot remember a post-game party when the band did not cover the classic "My Girl" by the Temptations. Our inspiration, though, came from the Tams song, "Be Young, Be Foolish and Be Happy."

After the party in this chaste period, dates were escorted back to dorms or sorority houses and brothers returned to guard the statue of a lion that stood in the front yard of the SAE house. Tradition inspired the rest of the FSU student populace, and quite a few adventurous townies, to try to paint our lion. Punishment for captured lion painters was a haircut administered by the SAEs.

Lifetime friendships were forged among fraternity brothers who spent post-game nights sitting in bushes or trees—guardposts in the weekly wars with would-be lion-painters.

Symbiosis requires mutual benefit and these glorious Saturdays help football as well as fraternities.

For many brothers, four undergraduate falls are too fleeting. So they return to campus year after year, buying season tickets, making annual donations to the Bulldog Club and other booster groups. I can keep up with old fraternity brothers through Seminole Club rosters - noting who has prospered enough to become a Golden Chief.

Although I live far to the north now, it is a rare autumn afternoon that I don't long to be back in Tallahassee when the Seminoles play at home, and after the game, dropping by the SAE house where I misspent my youth.

Boot Camp at 56

Machine guns blasted away with blanks. Explosions sounded like mortars. Our CH46 helicopter sat down in a smoky landing zone.

Second platoon scrambled out the back. Lugging our backpacks, we lumbered past the rear propeller. "Hit it!" the sergeant screamed.

I dove to the ground and landed on briars.

"Run!"

I jumped up and ran.

"Get down!"

My Kevlar vest weighed me down. My battle helmet fell over my eyes.

"Move out!"

My hands were scratched and bleeding. Sweat melted my camouflage war paint so that droplets of green and brown splattered on the lenses of my bifocals.

I didn't remember boot camp being this painful my first time around.

But that was thirty-four years ago.

I was twenty-two when I went through Army basic training at Fort Benning in the fall of 1968. Now, at fifty-six, I was going through military basic training for news media at this sprawling, wooded, muddy Marine base.

In 1968, I was drafted. In 2002, I volunteered. My first boot camp lasted nine weeks; this one was seven days. But the central purpose was the same for both—to prepare me to do my job in a war without getting myself killed or endangering other American lives.

I spent my year in Vietnam as a soldier, albeit as an Army journalist writing for military publications. If the United States goes to war in Iraq, I would go as a civilian reporter. The aim this time is to "embed" into a combat unit so I can chronicle the daily lives and missions of its members.

More than 400 journalists applied for this first media boot camp conducted by the Defense Department. The initial fifty-eight that were chosen represent thirty-one news organizations, ranging from the major TV networks to Russia's ITAR-Tass news agency. Several more such training sessions are planned in coming weeks.

But this one was mine to endure.

As the copter lifted off behind us, Second Platoon straggled to the tree line. Angel Franco, a Pulitzer Prize-winning photographer for The New York Times, had sprained his knee. Soon to be on crutches, he was our first casualty. He would not be the last.

As we panted and perspired in our gear, our platoon leader, Marine Captain Nicole Dube, warned the nine of us that endurance is vital for survival on the battlefield.

"When you're tired and don't want to run any more, you've got to ask yourself, 'Am I willing to sit and die right here?'" she said.

I resolved to turn the treadmill up several notches and hit the free weights hard when I returned to the fitness center in my office building in Washington.

To begin, we reported to the Pentagon at 0700 on the cold, rainy Saturday morning of November 16. Torie Clarke, the Defense Department spokeswoman, explained that one point of the exercise is to lessen the mutual mistrust that exists between the military and the media.

The training would begin on Navy ships and then move to the Marine base. Sipping a Starbucks coffee, Clarke said with a nearly straight face that she wished she could spend the week with us.

A few hours later, after a flight from Andrews Air Force Base, we found ourselves trudging through rain and sand on a North Carolina beach. There we boarded three LCACs—pronounced "el-cacks" and an acronym for Landing Craft Air Cushioned—to reach the USS Iwo Jima, which waited 25 miles out in the Atlantic.

LCACs are hover craft that take Marines from ship to shore for battle and then back out again.

The rain pelted down. Waves were five to seven feet. The LCAC bounced up and down, rocked and rolled.

I was sweating bullets.

Already seasick, ABC TV corrrespondent Dan Harris and I shared a seat behind the driver and navigator while a score or so of our colleagues sat below.

I clutched a plastic bag and stared at the gray horizon. It was hopeless. Soon I was heaving into the bag. That was too much for my seatmate, and his face went into his bag.

An eternity of misery later, the LCAC reached the entrance through the side of the Iwo Jima, an amphibious assault ship used to transport Marines.

I stepped aboard carrying a bag of vomit.

"You can leave that here, sir," a sailor said discreetly.

For nearly three days, we toured ships—ranging from a submarine to an aircraft carrier. We visited a brig, several bridges, flight decks, hangar decks, ward rooms, and even an "aft soda machine." We underwent drills for "man overboard" and "general quarters."

Secretive Navy SEALS showed us weapons and a mini-sub, then sold us T-shirts and caps.

On Monday evening, we arrived at Quantico. Our hosts eyed us skeptically.

"This is not a dog-and-pony show," warned Brigadier General George Flynn, commander of base training. Our time of "clean sheets and hot meals" had ended, he said.

At 5:00 A.M. Tuesday, platoon sergeants banged on our barracks doors.

This part of basic training was familiar, even after three decades. Only this time, I was politely called "sir" and "mister."

The all-volunteer force is far more motivated and better trained than were many of us reluctant warriors of the Vietnam era. These guys want to be here.

"It's even better than I thought it would be. It's awesome," said Sergeant David Alverson, our platoon sergeant. He turned eighteen in boot camp and now, at twenty-four, has no intention of leaving the Marines.

The threat of chemical or biological weapons of mass destruction being used in Iraq is much greater than it was in Vietnam. So on Thursday, after several hours in a classroom learning how and when to use a gas mask, we donned protective suits and set out to test our skills.

Flopping along in one-size-fits-all disposable rubber boots, we reached a cinder block building called a "confidence chamber." It was filled with a tear gas used in riot control.

This was the drill: The platoon enters the chamber wearing gas masks. We walk around showing ourselves that they work. We shake our heads to show that the seal withstands movement. Then we shut our eyes, hold our breath, break the seal, and let in some tear gas. Then we clear the masks. The gas burns our cheeks, but it's not bad.

Then came the big test. Again holding our breath and shutting our eyes, we remove the masks completely and hold them at our waists. Upon command, we put them back on, adjust the straps, clear the gas out, then secure the seals.

With eyes closed, I inhaled a whiff of the gas and received a bit of help straightening the straps. But it wasn't that bad. A couple of colleagues fared worse and fled the chamber early.

For the remainder of the training, we practiced seriously and put on our masks when an instructor yelled "Gas! Gas! Gas!"

"This is deadly serious," they told us.

We agreed.

On Friday, a five-mile hike in full field gear—dubbed the "media crucible"—concluded our training.

The test was altered somewhat after the International Herald Tribune published a picture of a reporter among us aiming a weapon at a firing range. We had not fired anything, but the impression aroused concern.

CNN, Fox News Channel and other TV networks covered our final hike. If we wore Marine gear as planned, an international audience might get a dangerous misimpression.

In parts of the world where we will be working, American journalists already are suspected to be spies, said John Kifner, a veteran war correspondent for The New York Times. TV images of reporters wearing military combat gear could create a real danger.

So, in varying degrees, we wore our own gear for the televised march. I wore the Marine Kevlar vest —which protects against shrapnel but not bullets—and carried the Marine gas mask. But I humped my own backpack and wore a cap instead of the combat helmet.

TV camera crews shot us along the route. At irregular intervals, we were hit with mock attacks. When the explosions sounded and smoke appeared, we scrambled into the woods. When instructors yelled "Gas! Gas! Gas!" we shut our eyes and held our breath and struggled to put on our gas masks within the prescribed nine seconds.

During one such ambush, we sustained a casualty when Richard Sisk, a New York Daily News reporter and Marine Corps veteran, landed on a flare and burned his hand. This time, the cry of "corpsman" was for real.

One correspondent started worrying about his pounding heart and called his cardiologist on his cell phone.

Meanwhile, sweaty and proud, the rest of us hiked up the final hill and reached the waiting media circus.

"I didn't think some people would make the hump today, but everybody did it," Captain Dube told Second Platoon. "Nobody fell out."

Even Franco, still on crutches, cheered us from along the route.

As for me, I had survived another boot camp. At this rate, I'll be ninety years old when my next one comes along.

"Mr. Dart," Captain Dube told me, "you were a trooper."

~

INDULGENCES

~

Fat Tuesday in the Big Uneasy   *Photo by Rick McKay*

Halfrubber

When half-baked by the sun and half-sloshed from the beer, the tourists figure hitting half a ball with a mop handle won't be a half-bad way to while away an afternoon at the beach. But they quickly find that it's wholly hard to do. Hence the appeal of halfrubber. The strange-sounding game is a laid-back, Dixie-fried version of the stickball relished by big-city Yankees. Only it is played under backyard live oaks or on sandy shores and with half of a rubber ball that curves, jumps, dips and dances when properly pitched.

The traditional "bat" in halfrubber is the wooden handle of a mop or broom, no more than forty-four inches long. The "ball" is solid sponge rubber, about the size of a baseball sliced in half.

Halfrubber is part of the heritage hereabouts. Since its origins in the alleys of Savannah in the early years of the Twentieth Century, the game has been passed from father to son for generations along the Georgia and South Carolina coasts.

The twelfth annual World Invitational Halfrubber Tournament in Savannah in September will draw teams from as far as Brunswick, Georgia, or Charleston, South Carolina, and maybe as far inland as Statesboro, Georgia. But that's it.

"Halfrubber is only played within a 75-mile or 100-mile radius of Savannah," said Pearson DeLoach, athletic director of the city's Leisure Services Bureau.

It's not much territory, considering that the eastern half of a circle with Savannah as the center is mostly Atlantic Ocean. This saltwater is considered home-run territory for halfrubber players on the beach. Batters usually face the surf and let sand dunes or seawalls serve as backstops.

Backstops are vital because a fast, curving, sidearmed halfrubber is nearly as hard for a catcher to snag as it is for a batter to hit. A good pitcher throws a halfrubber about 70 mph, and aerodynamics makes it veer sharply in almost any direction as it reaches home plate. "Hitting a halfrubber is much tougher than hitting a baseball," former major leaguer Ken "Hawk" Harrelson told Sports Illustrated. "You've only got half a ball to hit."

Harrelson grew up playing halfrubber in Savannah. "We used to play all the time on the beach," recalled DeLoach. "He's probably our most famous player."

Sports Illustrated, incidentally, covered last year's World Invitational Halfball Tournament. The resulting article cited "halfrubber's slightly raffish name" as a possible reason that the game has not gained wider popularity.

Through the decades, there has been considerable conflict over whether halfrubber originated in Savannah or Charleston, two cities that take their history seriously and are less than 100 miles apart. In his book, "Halfrubber: The Savannah Game," Dan E. Jones concludes that the game was first played in the Georgia port city.

"The game 'migrated' from Savannah to Charleston and not vice versa," Jones declared flatly. DeLoach, a lifelong halfrubber player, said the game evolved around the turn of the century from a pastime of Savannah firefighters, who played "baseball" with metal bottle caps and broomsticks while awaiting alarms.

From the flat, round bottle caps, it was a short step to halving a rubber ball to create two semispheres that could bedevil batters when pitched well. Legend has it that seventeen-year-old Charles Barbee borrowed a razor from his pal, Charlie George, and created the first halfrubber on a Sunday morning in 1913 on West Broad Street in Savannah. A version of the game is also played in Boston, only there it's called "halfball." The rules are different, though, and the halfball is cupped.

In his book, Jones points out that the Boston Red Sox trained in Savannah in the 1930s, and some of the major league players learned to play halfrubber during their stays. Ironically, Harrelson, who developed his batting eye playing halfrubber as a boy in Savannah in the 1950s, would later spend his best baseball years with the Red Sox. The enthusiasm for halfrubber tournaments has risen and ebbed over the decades, but the popularity of playing for fun has stayed as steady as the tides.

This year's World Invitational Halfball Tournament is set for September 9-10. Last year's tournament attracted twenty-five teams from places such as Hilton Head, South Carolina, Glenville, Georgia, and, of course, Savannah and Charleston. "Charleston teams have dominated the last four or five years," admitted DeLoach.

Indeed, last year, the finals were played between two Charleston teams: the Old Side and the Carolina Coot Hounds. The Charleston Old Side won 9-4.

But for most players, halfrubber is more an informal affair for hot, lazy afternoons than for organized, hard-fought competition. Games evoke memories as the obscure, seemingly ingrained skills required for halfrubber spring mysteriously back into action after long layoffs. A player recalls how his father taught him how to snap his wrist to control the curve of a halfrubber, and he passes the knack on to his own offspring. Old friends gather from afar at the same beach, year after year, to reminisce and compete.

Along this short stretch of coastline, halfrubber is as much a part of summer as beach music, skimboards and the Shag. Now, a trio of beachgoing entrepreneurs are attempting to take halfrubber commercial and spread the game's fame. Ricky Prevatt of Savannah and Dave Blackmon and Peggy Hibbs of Charleston have formed a firm to manufacture halfrubbers and bats.

Why would anyone buy a halfrubber when they can buy a rubber ball and easily make two?

"Ours is superior to the homemade version," said Prevatt. However, he said the real spur to begin the business was that "a three- inch rubber ball was getting hard to find."

Prevatt said he once spent two hours at Daytona Beach, Florida, in an unsuccessful search for a suitable rubber ball to slice. "My wife was mad because she thought I'd been driving around looking at girls," he recalled.

The experience prompted production of halfrubbers that sell for about a dollar and "don't break or tear up" when hit, said Prevatt. A halfrubber bat made of white ash and featuring a tapered handle was later put on the market.

"We're hoping to take this thing nationwide," said Prevatt.

Cheerwine and Such

It was 1917 when a slick-talking salesman from St. Louis stopped by a grocery store in Salisbury, North Carolina, and sold the peculiar cherry flavoring to L. D. Peeler.

Up until that time, in addition to selling foodstuffs, Peeler had been producing and bottling a carbonated soft drink called MintCola, which had been formulated in Tennessee.

But L. D. Peeler had a notion that North Carolina hankered for a cold taste of wild cherries. So he mixed the St. Louis flavoring with some sugar and other ingredients into a bubbly, burgundy-colored concoction he called Cheerwine (although it was not alcoholic).

In the three-quarters of a century since, the fame of Cheerwine has spread east to the Outer Banks and west to the Great Smoky Mountains. It's marketed with slogan "The Taste That's . . . Um . . . Hard to Describe" and has been dubbed "the nectar of the Tar Heels."

Peeler's great-grandson, Mark Ritchie, still uses the same secret family recipe and still makes Cheerwine concentrate only in Salisbury.

Such beloved regional soft drinks bubble up across the South.

Kentuckians are just as partial to Ale-8-One as Carolinians are to Cheerwine. In Tennessee, folks around Chattanooga wash down their Moon Pies with a Jumbo Orange. Some Texans allow that a Big Red goes mighty good with chicken-fried steak and cream gravy. In Virginia's Shenandoah Valley, Hoko Chocolate is a favorite. And all across Dixie, adventurous kids know there's nothing like a big ol' Double Cola that you fizz up with a handful of salted peanuts dropped into the bottle.

Iced tea, presweetened of course, is the South's most prevalent beverage. Moonshine is the most romanticized. Tennessee sipping whiskey, Kentucky sourmash bourbon, Florida orange juice and homemade scuppernong wine have all gained considerable fame throughout Dixie and beyond.

Even Gatorade is a Southern beverage, having been invented by a University of Florida physician for the school's football team.

But perhaps because bootleggers and Baptists kept their sweltering region legally dry for so long, Southerners have shown a distinct affinity for creating carbonated soft drinks.

"A number of brand name beverages originated in the South and have gone on to enjoy wide popularity," John Egerton points out in the *Encyclopedia of Southern Culture.*

Of course, Coca-Cola tops the list. It was created in 1886 by Atlanta pharmacist John S. Pemberton.

A year earlier, however, Charles Alderton mixed up the first Dr. Pepper in Waco, Texas, and named the drink for his mentor, Dr. Charles K. Pepper of Rural Retreat, Virginia.

Caleb D. Brandham, a pharmacist in New Bern, North Carolina, created Pepsi-Cola in 1896. Two years later, Edward A. Barq made the first Barq's Root Beer in Biloxi, Mississippi. In Columbus, Georgia, RC Cola was developed in 1933 as the successor to a ginger ale called Royal Crown.

Other Southern soft drinks, such as MintCola and Kentucky's Roxa Kola, went flat financially and disappeared into memory.

And some thrive in small, thirsty locales—developing a loyal following that's almost like a cult.

That's the situation with Ale-8-One of Winchester, Kentucky.

"We sell primarily in Kentucky," said Riley Rogers Walton, vice president of the beverage company founded by her grand-uncle. "But we're thinking of expanding to southern Indiana.

How popular is the pale gold ginger ale in green bottles?

The local newspaper reported recently that someone broke into a Winchester house and "stole one bottle of Ale-8-One."

Military sons and daughters of Kentucky had their parents ship cases of Ale-8-One to Vietnam and to the Persian Gulf during Desert Storm.

The Foodmart in Boonesboro, Kentucky sells eighty cases of Ale-8-One per week compared with four of Pepsi and two of Coke.

Once again, the recipe is a family secret, first mixed by G. L. Wainscott in 1926. The name "Ale-8-One" was conjured up in a local contest—apparently as a variation of "A Late One," although nobody can explain the pun nowadays.

Descendants of Wainscott still run the company. Local enthusiasts laud the drink's propensity to "keep you going" as well as its taste. The owners dispute the perception that the ale has unusually high concentrations of caffeine, although the earliest labels boasted of its "bracing pep."

Of course, folks in North Carolina attribute the popularity of Ale-8-One to the fact that Cheerwine can not be found in Kentucky.

Fruitcake

Down the road a piece in Jesup, folks claim that money smells like the smoke that belches from the Rayonier Paper Mill that provides most of the jobs in the southeast Georgia town. Up in Akron, Ohio, they say that money has the odor of burnt rubber like the tire factories that employ much of the populace.

Hereabouts, though, the citizenry knows that money smells sweet—like the sugary aroma that wafts along Main Street when Albert Parker and his family are baking fruitcake.

For more than half a century, this small town nestled within the piney woods and tobacco fields has been nearly synonymous with the holiday dessert that some folks love and some folks love to laugh at. This is the place where mass production assures that there is not just one fruitcake in the world that people keep passing around as a Christmas gift.

Indeed, they turn out about 86,000 pounds of fruitcake a day in Claxton.

The bakery that made the town famous—or infamous, depending on your affinity for fruitcake—sits two blocks off Highway 301, beside the Evans County courthouse, near the First Baptist Church and across from the railroad tracks. It's there that the Parker family makes the confection that has become a Christmas tradition in countless American homes.

"From September to Christmas, we do ninety-five percent of our business," said Albert Parker, the patriarch of the fruitcake clan. "We make cake year round. We sell it along the interstates at Stuckey's and do mail-order business. We sell it any way we can, but the majority of our business is at Christmas."

That business will produce and sell about seven million pounds of fruitcake this year and bring in revenues of more than $8 million. It's the largest "quality fruitcake" operation in the world, said Parker.

The red and white box, with its horse and buggy logo and the reassuring message that the cake is "baked in the Deep South according to a famous old Southern recipe," is among America's most familiar packaging.

That "old Southern recipe" calls for pineapple from France, citron from Puerto Rico, cherries from Oregon, Michigan or France, raisins from California, lemon and orange peel from Italy as well as pecans from Georgia.

And Claxton ships fruitcake worldwide.

"We sell a lot of cake in Canada," said Parker. "And we're working on our export business in Saudi Arabia."

This all started in 1910 when Savino Tos, an Italian immigrant, moved from Savannah to Claxton with his wife, Ethel, who was from Georgia. The couple opened a bakery and sold a variety of wares—ice cream, cakes, breads and buns.

During holidays, the bakery made and sold a colorful fruitcake that was somehow festive and reverent—like Christmas itself.

"Hold a thin slice up to the light and it resembles a stained glass window in a church," the baker Savino Tos would say.

The cake grew in popularity with the farmers, merchants and turpentine dippers of the region.

In 1927, Tos gave a job at the bakery to an 11-year-old local boy named Albert Parker. He worked after school and during the summers—sweeping up, churning ice cream, kindling fires in the brick ovens, learning the trade.

In 1945, Parker bought the bakery from Tos. He decided to specialize in fruitcake—a fateful choice.

That first year, they baked 5,000 pounds of fruitcake. The family has produced more fruitcake every year since, until now the annual production tops seven million pounds.

"I never expected it to grow like this," Parker admits.

The fruitcake sold well in Savannah and at roadside stands. But the Claxton Fruitcake got its biggest boost in 1952 when a businessman from Tampa drove through the town and stopped and bought a fruitcake.

He liked the taste and thought that his Civitan Club could sell the fruitcakes in its fund-raising drives. The cakes sold so fast that the International Civitan Club adopted the fruitcakes. The Civitans now purchase and then resell several million pounds of Claxton fruitcake per year.

Parker said the Claxton Fruitcake company has never even put a salesman on the road to drum up business. "We've always let the product speak for itself," he explained.

The fruitcake is baked in seven ovens in a plant that sits on the site of the immigrant's original bakery. It is still a family business. The sons and daughter of Albert Parker are all involved.

He is loyal to his product.

"A day hardly passes that I don't eat a slice of fruitcake," he declares.

South of the Border, South Carolina, 1985

Taj Mahal of Tourist Traps

The heyday of the Southern tourist traps is long gone now, driven into memory by the high-mileage, limited-access interstate highways and the proliferation of nationally franchised restaurants and motels.

Good taste, some argue, also hastened their demise.

Most of the roadside rips were temples of tackiness. Their coming was heralded for miles by the billboards that lined U.S. 17 and U.S. 301 and the other two-lane avenues to Florida that the Yankee tourists traveled each year.

"Alligator Farm. Florida Orange Juice. Georgia Pecans. Souvenirs. Clean Rest Rooms. Fireworks." The billboards were miles apart at first, then increased in frequency until the final one proclaimed: "Here It Is. Stop Now." The places were always disappointingly small. There might be a few caged animals in the "zoo" out back, but the real attractions were found in bins and shelves inside. Rubber reptiles. Genuine chenile bedspreads. Homemade pecan candy. Guava jelly. Cherry bombs. Jackets with embroidered flamingoes on the back.

For decades, these stop-offs were where Northern dollars were distributed through the South.

Most are gone now, though their kudzu-covered shells can still be seen on the stretchs of lonesome highways that wind between towns like Woodbine, Georgia, and Yulee, Florida. But a few of these economic dinosaurs of a bygone Dixie survived, even flourished, through the right mix of location, advertising, products, reputation and downhome gall.

One of the winners—in fact, a multi-million dollar winner—is here alongside Interstate-95 in the flat northeastern section of South Carolina.

This is not a subtle enterprise. The purpose of the massive, multi-colored Mexican hat 220 feet above the coastal plain is to complete the magnetic pull on metal automobiles traveling innocently along the interstate. Miles and miles earlier, the process of attraction had begun with roadside signs so silly that you actually anticipate the next outrage.

By the time the startling Sombrero Tower leaps up on the horizon, the tired drivers and car-cooped kids on I-95 have been hooked by Pedro's pitch for South of the Border.

They've seen Pedro presenting a giant fish with a halo advertising "Virgin Sturgeon" and "Unused Bagels." They've seen Pedro's "once in a blue moon" sign with "once" printed in a blue moon.

Stop, friends, at South of the Border and have a ball; Pedro's sign has a gigantic basketball stuck on it. And there's Pedro's "Smash hit" sign with what appears to be a real wrecked car fastened to it.

The kids and moms and dads have seen the strangely hued "horse of a different color" and Pedro's Mexican chimp saying, "No monkey business. Joost Yankee panky." They've read Pedro's weather report: "Chilli today. Hot tamale."

The signs broke their boredom and whetted their curiosity. Then the Sombrero Tower pulls them in pronto. Pedro always wins.

Welcome to South of the Border, the Taj Mahal of tourist traps.

If your children can read and if your route takes you on I-95 between the Carolinas, you're going to stop here. So relax. Buy a souvenir sombrero ashtray from Pedro for only $1.95. Eat some rainbow sherbert. Ride the elevator to the top of the sombrero. Look around. And marvel.

In a measurement designed for yesteryear's alligator farm, peach stand or fireworks emporium, South of the Border is off the scale. Sprawled over 130 acres, it is located just south of the border between North and South Carolina - hence, the name. It is touted in the state's tourism brochures. It's got its own exit from I-95. It even has its own dot on the road map - flat on one side because South of the Border is so close to the state line.

South of the Border also has a 304-room motel, seven restaurants, the El Drug Store, Pedro's Pantry grocery store, three swimming pools, an assortment of statues, miles of neon, a saloon, the S.O.B. water tower, a sewage treatment plant, a miniature golf course, a multi-brand gas station and an amusement park called "Amigoland" featuring a real antique train. There's a huge public restroom with paid attendants and coin-operated toilets, a 100-site campground, a bank, a volunteer fire department, a post office and, of course, the fourteen retail shops where tourists can buy anything from bullwhips to Elvis statues.

"On a good, steady day," said Alan Schafer, the seventy-one-year-old owner and founder of South of the Border, "about 25,000 people will stop here." On an average day, he said, somewhere between 10,000 and 15,000 people will go to South of the Border. The only "slow season" is between Labor Day and Christmas.

It all started in 1949, this only-in-America success story.

Alan Schafer, born and reared here in Dillon County, South Carolina, was a wholesale beer distributor in this Pee Dee River region of palmettoes and pines that straddles the border of the Carolinas. Then, Schafer recalled in a recent interview, several of his North Carolina counties voted themselves dry. He decided to build a little beer joint just across the state line in South Carolina to take care of thirsty customers.

Some local politicians asked him to sell some food along with his beer to make his place more acceptable to the neighbors, Schafer said, so he stocked hot dogs and hamburgers. He got the name of his new road-side restaurant from the directions contractors gave to reach it: "It's just south of the border."

There was no interstate highway around here back then. The original South of the Border sat beside U.S. 301.

But right from the start, Schafer said, he was amazed at how many hamburgers and hot dogs he sold.

"Then we found out that we were the only place on the highway between Fayetteville, North Carolina, and Florence, South Carolina, that sold hot food," he said.

Beer distributor Alan Schafer was abruptly in the tourist business, placed almost by providence about midway between New York and Miami.

South of the Border expanded, adding facilities and spreading like a commercial amoeba. Schafer began his own billboard shop and invented Pedro to spread the word from Georgia to Virginia. "Confederate cooking—Yanqui style," one sign said. "Yanqui prices, Pedro style."

"I wrote the copy," said Schafer. "It became sort of a hobby."

By the late 1950s, when I-95 was about to be built through the area, South of the Border was a travelers' institution, employing about 400 people on tourist dollars. Then Schafer heard that the I-95 interchange would bypass South of the Border. He said he went up to Washington and convinced the highway officials to re-route I-95 to prevent the loss of jobs.

"That was during the Eisenhower Administration," Schafer said. "And I've always been a Democrat so there couldn't be any accusations of political favoritism."

Such thoughts might arise because Alan Schafer is just about as controversial hereabouts as he is colorful.

He was recently released from prison after serving about 18 months for convictions on voting irregularities. The case involved absentee ballots and mail fraud. He was the county Democratic Party chairman for decades, Schafer explained, and got into trouble with federal authorities for his activities in a local election.

Another time, Schafer said, his creation of this pseudo-Mexican community hosted by the stereotypical Pedro was criticized by some actual Mexicans. Schafer recalled a letter of complaints that he got from the Mexican ambassador in Washington.

"I wrote him back and told him it was only tongue-in-cheek," said Schafer, explaining that he also mentioned how many Mexican-Americans he employs and how much Mexican merchandise he buys every year for South of the Border.

Schafer is also proud that his was among the first highway facilities in the South to open its doors to blacks during the segregation era.

"If they had U.S. dollars, we took them in," he said. "It cost us some white customers at the time, but it was the right thing to do."

Now, South of the Border is one of the major industries in the region, employing about 600 people, and Alan Schafer is a local legend.

"A lot of people give him credit for getting I-95 to run through Dillon County," said a long-time resident of the nearby town of Dillon, South Carolina. "He's a brilliant man, a multi-millionaire. It helped him for the interstate to come here, but it also helped the whole county."

How has South of the Border prospered so while so many of its competitors died by the highways?

"We've basically just had to keep on improving," said Schafer, who listens to his customers and changes his facilities and billboards frequently.

"I go out almost every day and talk to them," he said. "I never identify myself. They think I'm a tourist, too. That way, I learn what they like about the place and what they don't like."

Schafer's three sons are involved in his business now, but he has hardly retired. He is at work most every day, still dreaming up messages for Pedro and overseeing the ever-expanding South of the Border. He also still owns a wholesale beer distributorship.

Products are imported from Mexico by the truckload. Billboards are overhauled regularly. Some of the messages are changed every year or so, Schafer said, although a few have been the same for thirty years.

The array of merchandise is amazing inside the purple, yellow, pink and green walls of South of the Border's shops. Leather holsters for $49.85. Pedro music boxes for $12.95. Hand- tooled leather golf bags for $350. Karate headbands for 75¢. Acres of assorted ash trays. Forests of T-shirts. Sweatshirts that say "I like my beer cold, my women hot and my cars fast." Real sombreros, felt and straw. A $240 statue of a giraffe. A wooden bull.

"Sorry. No refunds," a sign said. "But Pedro will exchange."

"The most amazing part of this business to me," said Schafer, "is the things the public will just stop off the highway and buy."

He said South of the Border sells $250 leather jackets almost as fast as they can be imported from Mexico. However, ash trays and T-shirts are still the top sellers, Schafer said.

So, lots of folks do just like Pedro's elephant sign suggests: "Fill your trunque with Pedro's junque."

The motel rooms are also regularly refurbished, Schafer said. The rates run from about $40 a night for a standard room to up to $95 a night for a suite. There are "honeymoon suites" available, too, according to Pedro's signs.

They, uhh, are "heir conditioned."

Tupperware: A Burp of History

Like leftovers sealed with a burp in a Tupperware container, Brownie Wise's lifetime of documents were recently preserved in the archives of the Smithsonian Institution's Museum of American History.

But it is hardly a typical Smithsonian entry, and Wise is anything but a mainstream honoree. A plumber's daughter born in Buford, Georgia, in 1913, Wise had the ingenuity and energy to make her mark on the national culture.

She created the Tupperware party.

If you are snickering, consider some ramifications of her creation: Somewhere in the world, a Tupperware party begins every two-and-a-half seconds. Nine out of every ten American homes have at least one piece of Tupperware. A company that was going broke trying to sell its plastic containers in hardware stores half a century ago had $1.1 billion in sales last year. Most of this business was racked up by 950,000 "independent salespeople" hawking the patented airtight containers to the 105 million people who attended Tupperware parties in the homes of their friends and neighbors.

What's more, a book published by the Smithsonian contends the Tupperware party advanced the cause of feminism in the 1950s.

With American men back from World War II, women had been pushed back into the home and out of the jobs they had filled during the war. Tupperware parties gave postwar housewives an outlet for their economic ambitions, according to Alison Clarke, author of "Tupperware: The Promise of Plastic in 1950s America."

As a divorced mother, Brownie Wise "was very insightful and sensitive to women's lives and lack of opportunity for employment," Clarke said in an interview. "She herself struggled throughout the '30s and '40s to find work."

The Smithsonian papers, pictures and movies from Wise and Tupperware inventor Earl Tupper are the foundation for Clarke's book and were archived last month. Curators are considering creating a Tupperware display in the museum itself.

Wise was able to create a cultural icon because she both understood and embodied the American dream. She preached and practiced a simple philosophy: "There is nothing wrong with wanting things."

Brownie Humphrey grew up poor in the South, wanting things her family could not afford. She met Robert Wise while attending the Texas Centennial celebration in 1936, and they married soon after. With the Depression hard upon Dixie, the newlyweds lit out for Detroit, where Robert Wise found a job on a Ford assembly line.

The marriage was an unhappy one and short-lived. Three years after their son Jerry was born, the couple divorced in 1941. By then, the industrious Brownie Wise had adopted the pen name "Hibiscus" and was writing a column for women in the Detroit News.

In the column, "Hibiscus" was a transplanted Southern belle who lived in a modern, well-furnished house called "Lovehaven" with her successful and adoring husband, "Yankee," and their infant son, "Tiny Hands."

The sentimental columns about marital bliss and conspicuous consumption contrasted starkly with Wise's real life. She and her son had been abandoned by her husband and were financially imperiled, according to the Smithsonian book.

To augment her writing income, Wise started selling Stanley Home Products. The company employed former housewives as saleswomen and encouraged them to push its wares through their social contacts.

Meanwhile, halfway across the country in Leominster, Mass., a former DuPont company employee named Earl Tupper was trying to design plastic for home use. In 1942, he invented a flexible plastic bowl with a "snap" lid that could be sealed securely after the air inside the container was released.

Tupper envisioned a "Tupperization" of the American home: Spills and odors would be eliminated, and leftovers would move up the food chain through use of the lightweight plastic containers with the airtight seal.

But America's housewives were unreceptive. Tupperware arrived in stores in the late 1940s, after the war ended, and languished on shelves.

After being hailed as a miracle material, plastic disappointed many consumers by cracking or being otherwise unreliable. Also, to be appreciated, the unique Tupperware lid and "burp" had to be demonstrated, and store clerks were not up to the job.

Although heavily advertised in magazines, by 1948 "stacks of Tupperware collected dust on the shelves of hardware stores across the United States," Clarke wrote.

Then Brownie Wise discovered Tupperware.

She purchased some in Detroit through a plastics dealer and began selling it along with her line of Stanley Home Products. Then she organized a group of saleswomen—she called them the "Patio Parties" team—and soon they were selling so much Tupperware that Tupper summoned her to Massachusetts.

After a series of meetings, Tupper decided to abandon all store sales. He hired Wise to set up a national distribution system using her "hostess" plan. A middle-aged single parent with no formal business training, Wise would head the newly formed Tupperware Home Parties Inc. to sell the line of plastic containers.

It was an immediate and spectacular success.

Working on commissions, Tupperware distributors—almost exclusively women—would recruit acquaintances to invite friends and neighbors to parties in their homes. At this quasi-social affair, the distributor would demonstrate Tupperware products and take orders. The "hostess" received Tupperware "gifts" for providing the home and customers.

With young families filling new suburbs across America, Tupperware parties quickly became a national institution. Without the parties, Clarke said, "Tupperware would have been a design failure—for sure."

Although still single, Wise began living a flamboyant Southern lifestyle similar to the one in her "Hibiscus" column. Corporate headquarters for Tupperware Home Parties would be a gleaming white building surrounded by 1,000 acres of gardens and lakes on the Orange Blossom Trail near Orlando.

Wise's own lakeside mansion in nearby Kissimmee was filled with the "modern" furniture of the '50s. There was an indoor swimming pool and a cabin cruiser docked out back. She drove a "Tupperware Rose"-colored convertible and kept a matching pink canary caged in her office.

Wise once was asked by a women's magazine if she had considered remarriage.

"Why should I?" she replied. "My work provides me with all the fun, excitement and emotional outlets I could ever want . . . It enables me to give other women in financial trouble the same chance I had to help themselves to happiness."

In 1954, she became the first woman to appear on the cover of Business Week magazine. The key to Tupperware's success was the women who recruited "hostesses" and enthusiastically demonstrated the product at parties, she told the magazine.

"If we build the people, they'll build the business," she said.

For motivation, she invited top distributors to elaborate Homecoming Jubilees.

At the 1954 jubilee, Wise dressed in Western garb and invited distributors to "dig for gold" on the grounds of the company's Florida headquarters. Issued shovels, the women dug out buried mink stoles, diamond rings and other loot—including a toy car to be exchanged for a real one.

The 1957 Homecoming Jubilee featured a "wish fairy"—complete with tiara and magic wand—who granted the wishes of top saleswomen.

Wise reveled in the glamour and materialism. But Tupper, a stern New Englander, thought such displays showed bad taste. He thought the publicity about the parties and jubilees was overshadowing the product itself, Clarke wrote.

In 1958, Wise left Tupperware with a $30,000 separation payment—a small fortune in those days—for what was called "semi-retirement."

Wise stayed near Kissimmee and worked as a marketing consultant for several cosmetics firms. She died at age seventy-nine in 1992. Part of her legacy is the Museum of Historic Food Containers near Orlando, which Wise created in the 1950s. It traces the history of cooking and food storage from Egyptian earthenware in 4000 B.C. to, well, Tupperware.

~

RUMINATIONS

~

Neurotic Birds of North Carolina   *Photo by Rick McKay*

The Bottle Tree

The bottle tree stands on an acre nearly as fruitful as the garden in Genesis.

Nearby branches bear pecans and persimmons and apples and pears and peaches and plums and figs. There are vines of muscadines and leaves of mints and rows of corn, okra, tomatoes, beans, potatoes, cucumbers and collards.

Amid this bounty stands the bald redbud tree. Its sawed limbs hold aged green Coke bottles and blue Milk of Magnesia vials and clear bottles once full of purple or orange NeHi soda.

David Driskell, the African-American artist, historian and collector, cultivates his roots in this garden.

He grows the sorts of victuals that have sustained him since his boyhood as the son of a preacher and sharecropper in the North Carolina mountains. He created the bottle tree to honor his parents and harken to his African heritage. Over half a century ago, his father buried these glass containers beneath a hickory tree on their family farm. The son dug them up and displays them at his own home.

Slaves brought over this way of revering the spirits of ancestors. Like Driskell himself, the downhome shrine sparkles with artistry and soul and history and a touch of humor.

When people walk by at dusk and ask about the bottle tree, a smiling Driskell says, he tells them it's a "spirit catcher" and watches them scurry down the sidewalk.

The gently teasing gardener is an imposing figure on the American art scene.

Atlanta's High Museum of Art is currently showing 100 works usually displayed in his three-story, yellow Victorian house just beyond the goldfish pool and rose bushes. "Narratives of African-American Art and Identity: The David C. Driskell Collection" features the work of sixty artists and will be on exhibit until September 24. The traveling exhibition contains less than a fourth of Driskell's collection, among the nation's most extensive private assemblages of African American art.

The exhibit is different in that the collector shares deep personal ties with many of the African-American artists whose works are displayed. For nearly five decades, he has accumulated artworks through exchanges as well as purchases.

For the gardener is an artist, scholar and curator as well as a collector. In 1998, Driskell retired as chairman of the arts department at the University of Maryland—culminating forty-three years of college teaching. His academic writings and catalogues are landmarks in the study of African-American art.

As an art historian, "David's work was really important," said Mary Schmidt Campbell, dean of the Tisch School of the Arts at New York University. "He really was pioneering and groundbreaking in this entire field."

As a curator, he has counseled Bill and Camille Cosby on their private collection for twenty years. He arranged works by African American artists in the Huxtables house on TV's "The Cosby Show." He advised the White House on purchases of paintings by African Americans.

His two-story studio, with African masks on the walls and his mother's rocking chair near his easel, is located behind his Victorian house. His paintings are displayed in galleries in New York and California and hang in a number of museum collections.

"David is a Renaissance man," Howard University arts professor Starmanda Bullock told the Washington Post.

"I think of myself first and foremost as an artist," said Driskell. "Most people think of the writings I've done and they say 'art historian.' Well, yes, that's fine. I did that more or less out of necessity. There wasn't the forum for African-American artists' work out there when I came along . . .

"Secondly, I think the larger element of my contribution has come through teaching . . .," he continued. "And thirdly, perhaps as an art historian—a curator who has been helping to redefine the field of American art."

~

He was born sixty-nine years ago in Eatonton, a rural community on the Georgia Piedmont. When he was five, his family moved near Forest City in western North Carolina, close to his mother's relatives. He lived much of his childhood in a sharecropper shack where newspapers sealed the cracks in the walls. He occupied a pampered family position, however, as the youngest of four children and the only boy.

His father was a farmer, a Baptist preacher and a creative craftsman. His bank was a homemade pine chest, lined inside and out with tin, that is now displayed with the other African-American artwork in his son's home. His mother wove baskets from reeds and pine needles. His own talents were recognized early by teachers who encouraged his drawing.

In 1946, his father bought a 13-acre farm, Driskell recalls, and built a house "from rocks and boulders that he lugged up from the creek." His son was similarly determined.

"I went to a four-room high school up in the mountains. The teachers emphasized that the way out of this was to go to college," he said. "Nobody told me the particulars so I just got on a train and went to college."

With money earned in cotton fields, he headed to Howard University in Washington, D.C., an educational mecca for ambitious black students in those segregated times. He came to campus with his high school report card and promptly learned that the application process was somewhat more formal.

"I proceeded to sit in on class without their permission and wrote home and told everybody that 'I'm in college'," he said.

He was admitted the following semester. He studied art and history and began his collection. He met Thelma DeLoach, a secretarial student, and they were married in 1952. They would have two daughters, Daviryne and Daphne.

In 1955, he graduated and got a job teaching art at Talladega College in Alabama. Several years later, he returned to Washington to teach at Howard and earn a graduate degree at Catholic University. From 1966 to 1977, he was chairman of the art department at Fisk University in Nashville, Tn., where he authored several influential catalogues on African American art.

From Fisk, he moved to the University of Maryland where he headed the art department until his retirement nearly two years ago. Since then, he has traveled with his exhibit and painted.

~

Sitting amid his art treasures, Driskell spins colorful stories.

"One of the joyous parts" of collecting for the Cosbys, he says, "is being able to go to auctions knowing that I didn't necessarily have a limit on what I could spend and knowing that other people did.

"I would act like it was my money and just enjoy it. I just kept my paddle up," he chuckles. "If (the Cosbys) wanted something, they said 'get it'."

But he knows an artistic bargain when he sees one. "That's a Matisse," he notes, pointing to an original linocut on one wall. "I paid $2.98 for it at a flea market in Alexandria."

Under questioning, he reflects on evolutions in American art in the second half of the twentieth century.

"I have seen many, many changes in regards to first of all the inclusion of African American art in what might be referred to as mainstream tradition," he said. "Certainly, now it is inconclusive to talk about American art without including the contributions of African Americans."

The changes can be seen in museums.

"When I walked through the three floors of the High Museum, I saw something that I had not seen before," he said. "There were a large number of works by African American artists but they were integrated into the whole of the collection. They were not set aside in a room like you find in most museums . . .

"I thought to see this at a Southern museum was very heart-warming . . . ," he said. "That's what I've been teaching and preaching all these forty-five years. It's American art."

Spanish Moss Is Neither

Among my children's favorite tales about their Dad's growing up in South Georgia is the epic about the War Against the Billy Goat Boys.

In one battle, the good guys covered themselves in huge mounds of Spanish moss and crept like giant gray turtles down the alley behind Brownie Johnson's house to ambush the gang with the goat.

"Didn't you know they would notice a moving pile of moss?" my kids squeal with every retelling.

"Don't y'all know moss is full of redbugs?" our mothers scolded as the attackers scratched for a week.

Spanish moss was as much a part of a 1950s boyhood in Glynn County, Georgia as gnats and grits and saltwater marshes. Moss provided roofs for forts, relief for bare feet on hot sidewalks, bases for vacant-lot ballgames, landing pads for leaps from trees, beards for backyard theater and fodder for mischief.

My children live too far north and too far inland to have much of an affinity for Spanish moss. In North America, Spanish moss is found only in the coastal plain that stretches from southern Virginia to eastern Texas beside the Atlantic Ocean and Gulf of Mexico, explains Robert Wyatt, a botany professor at the University of Georgia.

"It grows best in humid areas near swamps, characteristically draping live oaks," he says.

Technically, though, Spanish moss is not a moss.

"It's a flowering plant. Some people mistake it for being a moss or a lichen because of the gray color," Dr. Wyatt says. "But it belongs to the Bromeliacae family, the same family that pineapples belong to."

The scientific name is Tillandsia usneoides. It's an epiphyte—a plant growing on another plant—but not a parasite, which would tap the host plant for food and water.

Spanish moss is photosynthetic—producing its own food. It gets water from rainfall and moisture in the air—not from the water supply of the host tree. Flattened scales—which give it a ghostly gray color—help reduce water loss.

Southern literature is rife with references to it. In Dixiefied novels, moss is always draped from some gnarled oak like a gray beard or dancing ghostlike in a soft evening breeze.

According to the Encyclopedia of Southern Culture, Spanish moss "is particularly associated with Gothic imagery of the Deep South, suggesting romantic, mysterious and sometimes menacing events."

Less lyrically, our mothers were right: Spanish moss does provide a home for redbugs. "Chiggers and mites and redbugs all live in it," Wyatt says.

Presumably debugged, moss has been used as stuffing for mattresses and furniture and as a padding for packages. Some Southeastern Indian tribes used it to make clothing. Southern settlers fed it to livestock. Confederates used it to make rope during the Civil War. Cajuns in south Louisiana use it for Christmas decorations.

Along the Gulf Coast, Spanish moss seemed to be under eviron-mental distress a few years ago, says Robert Thomas, director of the Louisiana Nature and Science Center in New Orleans. "The general feeling is that it is starting to come back. The presumption was that air pollution was causing the decline."

The recovery might be tied to emission controls on cars or the use of unleaded gas, he says. "Or it might just be some natural cycle."

Exactly why Spanish moss is called that is a mystery, says Charles Reagan Wilson, a professor of Southern Culture at the University of Mississippi. It is not, and apparently never has been, grown in Spain.

In the New World, it grows mostly in regions explored and claimed by Spanish conquistadors: the Deep South, West Indies and some coastal regions of South America.

That may explain the name, Wyatt suggests.

Regardless, it has become as symbolic of the coastal South as tourist traps and shrimp boats.

Indeed, journalist James J. Kilpatrick has written of Spanish moss as a metaphor for its native region: "an indigenous, an indestructible part of the Southern character, it blurs, conceals, softens and wraps the hard limbs of hard times in a fringed shawl."

Marshes

Although I live far to the north now, home to me will always be here where the marsh grass grows.

"On the firm-packed sand. Free. By a world of marsh that borders a world of sea."

Southern poet Sidney Lanier wrote those words while sitting beneath a shade tree in my great-grandfather's front yard.

"Affable live oak, leaning low" is how the poet described it in "The Marshes of Glynn." There's a historical marker at the tree, which was dubbed Lanier's Oak and still stands at the edge of a great marsh plain.

The nearby house, built by the first William Robert Dart, is now home to the Chamber of Commerce.

The second William Robert Dart, my daddy, knows the marshes of Glynn about as well as anyone ever has, having fished for nearly seventy years in the tidal creeks that meander through the county's vast grassy mud flats. Like the fictional Tom Wingo in Pat Conroy's "The Prince of Tides," my brothers and I "grew up slowly beside the tides and marshes . . . ."

The saltwater and marsh grass were as much a part of our heritage as were our mother's fried chicken and football games at Lanier Field. Mama Dart, our grandmother, captured the greens and grays and blues of marsh and water and sky on oil paintings that now hang like family portraits in our homes.

As toddlers, we played with fiddler crabs in the ebb tide's mud. Much of my education was achieved on my Aunt Mattie's front porch swing—reading, daydreaming and looking out across the marshes. I regret that my children haven't spent long summer days swimming and crabbing like we did from docks that spanned the marshes, mud and water.

Georgia's coastal marshes are the "most laterally extensive in the world"—stretching five to ten miles wide, said Steve Newell, an ecologist at the University of Georgia's Marine Institute on Sapelo Island.

Saltwater marshes are smooth cored grasses—Spartina alterflora to the scientifically inclined. They grow on the East Coast from Canada all the way down to South Florida, where the marshes end and mangroves begin. The marshes pick up again where the mangroves end on the east coast of South America. Another species grows on the west coasts of both continents.

Georgia owes what Lanier called its "marvelous marshes" to an ideal coastal elevation and a fertile clay base that rivers such as the Altamaha and Satilla have carried down from the piney woods and piedmont. Because of environmental threats from industries such as paper mills and by development from Georgians who wanted homes overlooking the scenic expanses, the state has enacted laws to protect the marshes.

The great green plains of marsh are partially covered during high tides and have an ecological importance that surpasses even their cultural impact.

Smooth cored grass is "one of the most prodigiously productive plants on Earth," Newell said.

The marshes support an amazing assortment of other life. Largely through decomposition—the detritus food chain—it flows to a wide range of animals. In essence, their existence is based on little pieces of dead marsh.

"Blue crabs and shrimp get half of their nutritional material from marshes," Newell explained. Mullet, sea trout, red drum, shrimp, oysters, marsh hen and a myriad of other sea and land animals rely on the marshes.

It's a complex ecological system that's still being studied.

Since 1953, when tobacco tycoon R. J. Reynolds donated the land on Sapelo Island, Marine Institute scientists have been trying to "find the basic truths about how this marsh works," Newell explained.

Which is what Sidney Lanier also wondered as he sat in the shade of that live oak.

"And I would I could know what swimmeth below when the tide comes in

"On the length and breadth of the marvelous marshes of Glynn."

The Romance of Letter Jackets

The teenagers hereabouts call it "going out," as when my daughter informed me last year, "Ryan asked me to go out with him."

"Go out where?"

"Oh, Daddy," she said in exasperation. "It's what y'all called 'going steady' in the olden days."

Actually we called it "going with," but there was no need to quibble over such ancient history.

She figured I would like Ryan because he wore Topsiders with no socks and played linebacker on the freshman team.

It wasn't a bad start, I admitted.

But abruptly, after a quarter of a century or so, I had been thrust back into a subculture of Southern high school romance—fortunately as an observer this time around.

Surprisingly, many of the rituals are unchanged. Even in the '90s, it's a whirl of Weejuns and wrist corsages and flattops and sock hops and hours-long phone conversations. Call-waiting is a welcome technological advance.

The way they cruise Maple Avenue and socialize in the McDonald's parking lot seems a lot like the way we used to while away weekend evenings driving between the Pig & Whistle and Shoney's.

Some things are different in the hormonal New South. There were drive-in movies for our dates along coastal Georgia. Girls of the '60s rarely gave their boyfriends an earring as a token of affection. The issue of whether condoms should be distributed in the high school clinic never came up back then.

The geography is different too. There are no beaches here in the northern Virginia suburbs, so teenage boys presumably must come up with better lines than the "Want to go watch the turtles lay eggs?" that we tried on the tourist girls from Waycross or Tifton.

Of course, there probably are some changes a dad does not know about and might not want to.

But walk into the gym of Vienna, Virginia's Madison High for any basketball game and you'll see one true-love tradition that has survived in Dixie for decades—girls in boys' coats, about six sizes too big, with leather sleeves dangling about a foot past their fingertips.

High school jocks still give their letter jackets to the girls they are "going out with."

My "G" jacket from Glynn Academy went to a cheerleader, and I'm still amazed at how eagerly I offered it.

High school football practice has always been a special kind of hell down in the land of the boll weevil and Bear Bryant. I can remember contemplating chopping off a toe with an ax rather than suffer another August of two-a-days.

Redemption came on Friday nights and at season's end, when the letter jackets were awarded.

By January, though, the jackets were not being worn by the players who had spent months sucking in gnats during wind sprints and pushing a blocking sled until their thighs screamed.

Without breaking a sweat, girls had virtually all the football "G" jackets.

Now, decades later, at Madison High, it's the girls who are wearing the football players' "M" jackets.

What is surprising about the survival of this custom in the post feminist teenage subculture is that many of the girls already have letter jackets of their own.

Indeed, the Madison High girls have won state championships in basketball and softball in recent years while the football team has barely broken even.

It's sort of a high school truism here that playing a varsity sport looks good on a college application, so most girls run track or cross country or play tennis or field hockey or lacrosse or something.

I asked my daughter, who plays lacrosse, if a girl ever gives her letter jacket to her boyfriend.

"Oh, Daddy," she replied, rolling her eyes like she did the time I suggested she buy a pink boutonniere for her homecoming date.

Tobacco Barns

Like the Sunset Drive-in picture show and U.S. 17 tourist traps, the faded wooden tobacco barns of my Southern youth have rotted and tumbled into kudzu-covered memories.

"You still see a few of the old ones sitting around the countryside, but very few are used," allowed Phil Phillips, a fourth-generation tobacco farmer from Lynchburg, South Carolina. "Most remain just to remind ourselves of the way things used to be."

I remember how things used to be.

Throughout my childhood, my grandfather on my mama's side of the family grew tobacco in a hot, dusty field out beyond the fish pond on his farm in Jeff Davis County, Georgia.

Near the banks of the pond stood his tobacco barn, a tall structure with walls of weathered gray planks and a roof of galvanized tin. It stood silent and empty save for a few frantic weeks in late summer.

When time came to pick and cure the broad, sticky green leaves of tobacco, the barn bustled with activity as neighbors brought over their skills and gossip. Families helped each other during harvests.

In those days, the men would pick the tobacco leaves off the stalks and pile them into a long, narrow sled with burlap sides that was pulled behind a tractor. In earlier times, a mule dragged these sleds through the fields and to the tobacco barn.

A porch on the side of the barn provided shade for women who would use sturdy white twine to tie the tobacco leaves to wooden sticks. They were wondrously fast at this process, which was called "stringing tobacco." The tobacco sticks were actually rough-hewn lumber, one-by-one inches in girth and about six feet long.

The sticks with strung tobacco dangling below were hung from the barn rafters. Over the next week or so, dry heat was used to transform the green leaves into the aromatic, golden, flue-cured tobacco that would be taken off the sticks and trucked to auction.

When I was about seven years old, I spent several sweltering days picking bugs off the green leaves before they were strung on sticks. It wasn't much of a job, but it was enough to convince me to spend my summers playing Little League baseball and going to the beach instead of working in tobacco.

In the eleven months of the year that it was empty, the tobacco barn provided entertainment for my two brothers and me on our frequent visits to Granddaddy's farm. There were nests of wasps and dirt daubers to knock down. There were lizards to catch and snakes to avoid. Mostly, though, there were hundreds of tobacco sticks. We stacked them into forts or used them individually as swords or spears or staffs in our frequent battles. We limboed under tobacco sticks and high-jumped over them. We tried, unsuccessfully, to bind them together into a raft that would float us across the fish pond like Huck and Jim floated down the Mississippi.

In the high-tech agricultural South, however, the sticks and "conventional tobacco barns" have "gone the way of the boll weevil. They've almost been eradicated," said Donnie Smith, a third-generation tobacco farmer at Willacoochee, Georgia.

Today's "bulk barns" are made of metal. Tobacco is picked by machine and the leaves loaded into metal boxes while still in the field. These boxes are stacked in the bulk barns, where force-fed hot air dries the leaves.

"It's much more efficient," said Smith. "You can control the humidity and the temperature. And you use fewer people. You don't have to unstring the tobacco so it eliminates a lot of hand labor."

Examples of the conventional curing barns, complete with tobacco hanging from sticks, can be seen in two museums in North Carolina: the Tobacco Farm Life Museum in Kenley and the Duke Homestead State Historic Site in Durham.

Tobacco is a peculiarly Southern crop, tied to the region by climate and custom. Technology is not the only force challenging its dwindling ranks of growers from Virginia to northern Florida.

Faced with health hazards and increasing societal hostility to smoking, fewer Americans are using tobacco products.

In addition, anti-smoking forces in Congress and the public health community are pushing a sort of "backdoor prohibition"—continually raising taxes on cigarettes and eliminating places people can smoke—Smith complained. "Sometimes, I feel frustrated and angry. They want to take away my livelihood."

Indeed, there may come a time when the modern metal tobacco barns join their weathered wooden forebears under the creeping kudzu.

Neurotic Birds of North Carolina

Growing up in this textile mill town six decades ago, John Bradford was fixated on birds. He drew birds in grammar school when he should have been studying. He learned birdcalls. Whenever he saw a strange bird, he'd run home and look it up in the encyclopedia.

"But I never dreamed anything like this would happen," marveled Bradford, sitting amid the clamor and cages of a suburban house that has become a national asylum for neurotic, injured or neglected exotic tropical birds.

There are 215 feathered patients currently in residence. Human conversation occurs over a cacophony of squawks and shrieks and whistles reminiscent of an amplified sound track of a Tarzan movie. Particularly piercing is the voice of Ringer, a hyacinth macaw with a formidable feathered head and a naked torso that appears ready for the poultry section of a supermarket freezer.

Ringer is "a self-mutilator" with emotional problems that compel him to pluck his own feathers, explained Mary Bradford, whose ornithological interests are as strong as her husband's.

The Bradfords are birds of a feather, so to speak, and they have flocked together an amazing assortment of troubled fowl. Hyacinth macaws like Ringer, for example, are the world's largest parrots. Only about 1,000 remain in the wilds of Brazil and those bred in captivity sell for $5,000 to $40,000 in pet stores.

Orko, a Moluccan cockatoo with a self-plucked body, won $10,000 on "America's Funniest Home Videos" for the recorded reaction to his first encounter with a bald human. The Bradfords used the prize money to build an aviary in their back yard.

The original patient in what is now the non-profit "Tropics Exotic Bird Refuge" is Georgie, a blind, blue and gold macaw. He arrived by happenstance.

After years of longing, the Bradfords had saved up enough in 1990 to buy a feisty pet parrot named Moppet. The bird had bitten everyone but the Bradfords so the pet store owner was impressed with their handling skills. When Georgie's elderly owner could not longer deal with a blind parrot, she gave the pet to the store.

The store owners figured that "anyone who could handle Moppet could handle a handicapped bird," explained Mary.

Suddenly the Southern couple was operating a sanctuary. Word spread through bird clubs, magazines and Internet sites. Pet owners, zoos, breeders and storekeepers were soon dropping off birds with physical and mental problems at the modest, ranch-style house on the edge of Kannapolis. Seeking room for their growing flock, the Bradfords built two additions onto the house and then constructed two buildings out back. John, a retired commercial printer, did the work.

"Our dream" is a series of back-yard geodomes that will allow the birds to fly free within an environment similar to their native rain forests, said Mary. Meanwhile, operating funds come from bird-loving contributors and sponsors such as bird feed companies.

The sanctuary has been featured on Nickelodeon's "Nick News", a TBS National Geographic Explorer segment, the UPN Network's "America's Greatest Pets" and other television programs. Of course, the media attention brought in more requests for help from all over the country.

"We're dealing with birds that haven't adapted well" as pets, said Mary. Often calls come from frantic owners pleading "Come and get this bird before I kill it or turn it loose."

~

In a nation with an estimated forty million pet birds, there is no shortage of troubled tropical species.

The problems often begin when people buy a macaw or cockatoo or other large parrot on a whim, said Patrice Klein, the wildlife veterinarian for the Humane Society of the United States.

Since parrots can live up to 100 years, a conscientious owner will have made a lifetime commitment, said Klein. Too often, though, the person has no idea what the proper care of the new pet entails.

Dogs and cats have been domesticated over centuries of breeding for cohabitation with humans. To a lesser extent, so have parakeets and canaries. Not so the larger, exotic birds that in recent decades have become "popular and fashionable"—and expensive—pets, said Klein.

Even if hatched domestically, "they still have fairly wild characteristics and complex needs," she explained. It is illegal to import most of these exotic but endangered birds.

In their jungle homes, these large birds live in flocks and "are very social animals," Klein said. They often mate for life.

In captivity, therefore, the birds need hours and hours of interaction with their human owners. They can't be regarded as a living decoration. Without proper care and attention, Klein said, the birds can become "psychotic."

"Feather picking is a common behavorial problem among companion birds," said Barry Hartup, a professor of wildlife medicine at the Cornell University College of Veterinary Medicine. The causes can be physical—throid problems or parasites—but more often are emotional. A frequent cause is loneliness.

"Most parrot species are very social animals" and need stimulation from their owners or other birds, said Hartup.

Beyond their craving for attention, the birds bring other problems into the homes of their owners.

They are startlingly loud. Indeed, the Bradfords provide earplugs for visitors. The screeches that a parrot uses for jungle communications can quickly cause human headaches inside a house.

Even the intelligence of the birds can cause problems. "They are like a two-year-old child," said Klein. Parents often describe this as a difficult age for their children and it's no different with birds.

"They're always in 'the terrible twos' and they live for eighty years," said Klein.

∿

Beanie Babies birds are perched on Bradford's mantlepiece and real parrots fly freely within the house. There's a constant clean-up of feathers and poop. The noise is endless. Sometimes it seems that sanity has flown the coop.

"My sister thinks we're crazy," said John. "She says she couldn't live like this."

But the Bradfords have found satisfaction providing a home for birds that need one. They take a few of their charges out for educational lectures at schools, churches and community gatherings and they host field trips for science classes. Most of the birds welcome company.

Entering the backyard aviary, a visitor is greeted with choruses of "Hello," "Hello," "Hello," "Hello," coming from dozens of beaks. A single squawk sets off a chain reaction in cages across the large room.

"We always ask for their cages," said Mary. "The bird should move here with its own home and toys."

Walking through the aviary, John and Mary frequently open cages and take out the bird inside. Every bird has its own favorite form of play. A cockatoo might be cuddled like a baby, a parrot perched on a shoulder.

The variety of species make up a sort of loud, living rainbow. There are pink-breasted Bourke parakeets from Australia and African gray parrots and white cockatoos that bounce up and down and spread the feathers on their heads like an umbrella.

John points to a cage holding several multi-hued Quaker parakeets. "Some people think they make good pets," he said. "But they're like a feathered pit bull."

Birds that are still self-mutilating wear protective bandages and vests. Some have stopped attacking themselves but are permanently plucked—having destroyed the follicles from which feathers grow.

One cherry-headed conyer is almost completely bare of feathers. It began its own plucking and was later assisted by a companion bird that picked off the head feathers. The sad result is a bald, beaked creature that appears to have come from a cartoon.

Every bird here has a story. Tango lost a foot to frostbite after being left outside by a previous owner. A tempermental cockatoo was brought in by a couple afraid that the jealous bird would hurt their new baby. A parrot with clipped wings was paralyzed after falling from a perch.

For awhile, the Bradfords tried to find homes for the troubled birds. But they gave up after repeatedly having to "rescue them from the rescuers," said Mary. Now they hope to keep expanding to care for the needy birds that folks just keep bringing in.

The birds can't survive in the wild, said Mary, and would become "hawk bait" if set free.

So the Bradfords keep taking them in, knowing that usually the troubled birds have nowhere else to go.

~

JOURNEYS

~

The Santa Train   *Photo by Rick McKay*

The Santa Train

She always wanted to ride the Santa Train.

Growing up a coal miner's daughter, she stood beside the tracks every year awaiting the caboose carrying the jolly bearded man who tossed out candy and early Christmas presents to the children of Appalachia.

"We always took our paper pokes ('pokes' is an Appalachian term for bag or sack) and waited for the loud scream of the train and Christmas music," recalled Vickie Addington. "How forward we looked to this."

Even after her own children were grown and gone from this Critchfield Coal Company town, Vickie and her husband, Eugene, would be out with their neighbors every November when the train stopped here briefly on its cheerful journey from Pikeville, Ky., to Kingsport, Tenn.

Then, this fall, at the age of forty-seven, she was diagnosed with terminal cancer.

"My dream has always been to ride the Santa Train," Mrs. Addington confessed in a letter to the Kingsport Chamber of Commerce. Along with the CSX Railroad, the chamber has sponsored the annual holiday trip for fifty-seven years.

"I'm not begging," she stressed, for hard times forge proud folk. But it "would be my dream come true" to stand beside Santa and "throw candy to our Appalachian children."

"I don't require oxygen and only a few medications," she said. And Eugene would go along to help her.

"You can never imagine how great I would feel for the first time in a long while," she wrote. "Please allow us to go."

Well, only Grinches aboard a Scrooge Train would deny such a request. Of course, the sponsors welcomed Vickie and Eugene Addington to make the trip.

~

As it has for over half a century, the Santa Special rolled out of Shelby Yard around sunrise on the Saturday before Thanksgiving. It whistles past Marrowbone and Splashdam, rumbles through the coal fields and hollows, crosses over Copper Creek trestle and under Sandy Ridge tunnel, creaks past memorable miles of abandoned appliances, rusted house trailers and resilient smiles.

The goodies are loaded in Kingsport and taken on the train to Shelby, then distributed the next day on a jerky trek along the winding ridges and tumbling rivers where Virginia, Kentucky and Tennessee meet in a mountainous confusion of borders.

The merchants of Kingsport, spurred by commercial and spiritual reasons, fired up the first Santa Special in 1943.

"This didn't begin as a charitable effort," said Elaine Bodenweiser of the Chamber of Commerce. "From the start, it was a show of gratitude for shopping in Kingsport."

For some poor families in the hardscrabble hollows, though, those early trains brought the bulk of their Christmas cheer.

"We didn't get much candy otherwise," recalled Juanita Jackson, standing by the tracks in Elkhorn City, Kentucky, with her daughters, granddaughters and neighbors. Times are considerably better now, but the Santa Train is still a Jackson family tradition.

"We always get up at 6:00 A.M. to be here on time," lamented Amy Jackson, who came home from college in Roanoke, Virginia, for the event.

"It gets you in the Christmas mood," said Jean Vandyke, a Jackson in-law.

Over three decades aboard the Santa Train, Frank Brogden has seen "a substantial improvement in the lives of the people" who stand beside the tracks. Indeed, this year's gifts included "Lion King" videotapes for the children and "Denver Bronco Super Bowl Season" videotapes for their fathers. The sponsors figured that many mountain cabins have VCRs.

The train still rolls past some rusted carcasses of cars and ramshackle house trailers perched precariously on the rugged, wooded mountain-sides. But many families arrive at their favorite spots in new SUVs. Men wear camouflage fatigues and orange caps of deer hunting season. Women are dressed in jeans and holiday sweatshirts. Children are bright-eyed and well-scrubbed. The mood is nostalgic and festive rather than desperate.

Nowadays, "we focus on the tradition," said Brogden, a retired public relations executive who has served as Santa for the past seventeen years.

"I've been coming for the last forty years," said Valerie Damron, holding her grandson, Preston, as Santa threw out gifts at Dungannon, Virginia. "I brought my children and now my grandchildren."

"I remember snow and ice building up on my mittens as I waited by the track. I would get a little ruler and some pencils and some candy," said Colleen Massey, who grew up in Dante (which rhymes with "can't" hereabouts). She lives in Tennessee now, but returns each year to relive her childhood experience.

"When the train comes around the bend, the tears start flowing," she said. "It's so emotional and I enjoy it so much."

~

Vickie Addington bought a new hat for the trip after losing her hair to chemotherapy. Even her eyelashes fell out after the potent treatments.

She compared the moment that she heard her diagnosis of Non-Hodgkin's Lymphoma to the childhood moment when she heard that President Kennedy has been shot. "I was once again frozen in time," she recalled.

But in the following weeks, thoughts of her holiday trip eased her worries.

"She bought a new Christmas outfit to wear," said her husband. "Every day, she would tell me, 'We're going to ride that train'."

Living on a miner's pension after twenty-five years underground, Eugene Addington has Santa Train memories of his own.

"I was born the year the train began and I was at it every year. We lived beside the track," he said. "I always looked forward to getting those little pop guns."

~

The Santa Train is practically a year-round operation. This year, fifteen tons of candy and clothes and toys were distributed to thousands of people along the 110-mile route.

Contributed food and merchandise "comes in literally by the truck-load," said Miles Burdine, executive director of the Kingsport Chamber. The donated bounty is collected during the year at a supermarket warehouse. The head of collections is dubbed the "bummer."

Kingsport, with 36,000 residents, is home to Tennessee's biggest employer, an Eastman-Kodak plant that has 13,000 workers. With several other high-wage industries, the town is more prosperous than some of its neighbors.

Shortly before the trip, the presents are put into coded plastic bins—gray for foodstuffs, red for toys and clothes—and systematically arranged in railcars for distribution along the way. Santa and his helpers shouldn't run out of stuff to throw but also don't want anything left over at the end of their run.

The late Charles Kuralt did a CBS-TV "On the Road" segment aboard the Santa Train some years back and the worldwide attention and contributions have escalated since then. The monetary donations have reached a level to where the Chamber now awards a $5,000 college scholarship each year to a deserving high school senior who lives along the route.

CSX Transportation sends up special rail cars from its corporate headquarters in Jacksonville, Florida, for the trip and celebrities clamor to be a Santa's helper. Last year, country music star Travis Tritt made the trip. This year, Patty Loveless helped throw out the gifts.

"I saw some cousins," said the singer, who was born in Pikeville but moved away at the age of ten. "The hardest part was waving at them and not being able to stop and talk."

The scene was wild when the train would stop for ten minutes or so at a town and presents would rain down on the excited crowd.

Holding her grandson in Elkhorn City, Evaughn Campbell was hit in the forehead by the hard edge of a flying Little Golden Book. Two nurses rushed from the train to wash the blood from her face and dress the cut. Meanwhile, Santa's helpers kept the grandson happy with gifts.

Away from the settlements, though, families stood in isolated spots all along the route and waved at the passing train. "A dozen kids are coming up on the left," a spotter would yell on the platform behind the caboose. Santa and helpers would throw stuffed animals, Moon Pies, Barbie Dolls, Hershey Bars or any of a myriad of other goodies on the railbed.

Waving and shouting "Merry Christmas" as the train sped away, the children would scramble onto the tracks to pick up their presents.

Eight or more hours of throwing out presents and shouting "Ho. Ho. Ho." makes for "a very demanding day," said Brogden.

At the end of the trip, Santa leaves the train and boards a fire engine to ride in the annual Kingsport Christmas Parade.

～

Sadly, they buried Vickie Addington a few hours after the Santa Train passed through Dante on the Saturday before Thanksgiving.

Her death had come the night before she and Eugene were scheduled to board the train in Kingsport and ride to Pikeville to begin this year's journey.

"The last words she told me were 'I love you'," said her husband. "I found her dead in the bed."

Next year, he hopes to ride the train in the memory of his wife.

"She wanted to go so bad," he said.

The Ballad of Formerly Fat John Westbrook

First off, Fat John Westbrook ain't fat no more.

I got that straight from some North Florida boys who saw and heard him at an impromptu concert near Starke awhile back.

"They were celebrating the watermelon harvest," now-svelte John recalled last week at his home in St. Augustine. "We made a stage out of two bales of hay in the back of a Ford pick-up. I played from there, had a real good time. Passed a fruit jar and took in over $100."

John Westbrook is a long-time friend of mine. He's a guitar-picking songwriter, one of the breed Jimmy Buffett called "hungry, hard-luck heroes" in his classic ode to shoplifting tunesmiths "Who's Going to Steal the Peanutbutter?"—although Westbrook probably would take exception with the assessment.

"Actually I look like Kenny Rogers now," Westbrook said in self-appraisal. "My beard's gone gray."

He was never really fat, anyway. He was pretty big, a tackle on his high school football team, and Fat John was a fraternity house nickname. Like the fellow with the personality of a turnip who was dubbed "Veggie".

Westbrook and I hit it off right quick, probably because we were the only guys at the SAE house at Florida State who knew the words and yodels to "Lovesick Blues." Only he knew the tune, too, and could pick it.

We were also starters on the PBR team that held Thursday night scrimmages with a couple of cases of Pabst in order to warm up for the week-end. Somebody had borrowed a couple of hymnals from the Wesley Center and we'd end up singing "Rock of Ages" and "The Old Rugged Cross" before we headed to a subterranean bar known as The Keg where they had a band. Those are the things that build lasting friendships.

Westbrook tried to go straight after college. He even got a job as a stockbroker and wore suits. It couldn't last, though. He traded his Weejuns-and-Gants wardrobe for jeans, sandals and T-shirts and hit the road for musical fame and fortune. And freedom.

Naturally, he plays original stuff—not just country music, but rhythm-and-blues and native beach-folk-rock tunes from the Florida coast, as best I can figure. He's a storyteller

After an Army tour in Vietnam, I was prolonging my education in graduate school at the University of Georgia when Westbrook showed up in Athens one Sunday with his blonde wife and big black dog Magnolia for a two week gig at T. K. Harty's Saloon. I introduced them to my bride and they all slept on our floor.

T. K. Harty's wasn't the best place for a semi-serious singer to perform. It attracted a hard-drinking, pinball-playing crowd that mainly paid attention when Westbrook pulled out his banjo. Then they hollered and stomped. He tried playing some piano boogie but I think he was scared to turn his back on the audience for very long. There was no chicken wire barrier protecting the entertainment from flying beer bottles.

Mostly I remember a song about a gay biker gang in Key West that revved up their engines by putting playing cards in the spokes of their ten-speed Schwinns and scared tourists off the sidewalks. Another one had to do with a wife-killer who escaped from jail in Thomasville, Georgia, fled to Texas and happily ate tacos.

Westbrook said he doesn't sing those songs anymore. "My humor has gotten a lot more subtle," he explained.

When he left Athens, Westbrook gave me his last tie, swearing off on formal neckwear. I wore it on my first job as a reporter.

But John might have backslid. He sings in the choir at the First Methodist Church in St. Augustine now. Along with his Mama.

Westbrook has played beach bars from Key West to St. Simons, ventured inland to Nashville, even tried the North.

"I went hunting the elusive Yankee last year," he said. "Became a rock 'n' roll star in Lake Placid, New York."

He cut an album, sort of by himself, and has been looking for a label. He said he got the run-around from a company in Atlanta a couple of weeks ago.

The album is his stuff, he said, a raunchy sex song, an ode to St. Augustine girls, his own stories. He sells the records on his own, now, back at home with Magnolia.

I don't know if John Westbrook will ever become a star. I do know he's had the guts to give it a shot. I don't know if he's satisfied but he's always struck me as being happy.

There's a lot to be said for living your life like you want to.

～

Sadly, my friend John Westbrook died much too young in his beloved St. Augustine.

Discovering Daddies

It's Father's Day at The Wall.

The sons and daughters of the men whose names are chiseled on the polished black granite are themselves grown now. They bring their own children to hear stories of grandfathers they will never hug.

The Vietnam Veterans Memorial has always been a place of healing. So the grown-up sons and daughters weep and laugh and embrace each other and share memories of fatherless childhoods.

Army Captain William A. Branch's daughter, Jen, was a toddler when he was killed at Dau Tieng in 1970. Ever since, folks have told her, "Oh, you were only two. You didn't know him." Was it somehow better that she had no memories of her father? Didn't they know that left an emptiness inside her?

Captain Branch was buried at Fort Benning, Georgia, on a summer day thirty years ago. His wife came home from the funeral and saw their daughter astride a riding toy and thought, "She will never understand the kind of man that her father was."

But her mom was mistaken.

It's true that her dad and Vietnam were rarely mentioned when Jen was growing up in Atlanta. Her mother, a schoolteacher, remarried and there were strains enough within a blended family without a child's painful questions. But there was still that emptiness within.

So at eighteen, she followed her father's footsteps to North Georgia College, a school with a military heritage. Attending on a scholarship named for her father, she walked across drill fields where he had marched and she searched old yearbooks for his pictures. She talked to professors who had taught him and to his classmates who came to reunions. Many wore uniforms—their chests bearing a "fruit salad" of medals—and she wondered what career path her father would have followed into middle age.

Back in Atlanta, she searched an attic and found an Army footlocker packed with precious memories. There were cartoons that Bill Branch had drawn as a boy growing up in Fitzgerald, Georgia. He was always a gifted artist. As a battalion intelligence officer, he crafted wonderfully detailed maps in Vietnam. She found a treasure trove of letters. He had written her mom every day of two combat tours.

There was one to her:

"Darling Jennifer, I love you little girl. I keep your picture with me always. I'm coming home to you soon and I'll make up for lost time. I'm going to be the best daddy around ..."

Captain Branch's little girl is nearly thirty-two now—about two years older than he was when killed. Jen Branch Denard is married and lives near Fort Lauderdale, Florida. She has come to The Wall on Father's Days past but this time she brought her mother for a first visit. Wars cannot kill relationships, the daughter says.

"These men did not die for nothing," she believes. "Their spirit is living on in their children and their grandchildren and it will live on forever. Our responsibility is to make sure they are not forgotten."

⁓

Among the 58,209 Americans lost during the Vietnam War, about a third were fathers. Their deaths left about 20,000 children to feel hollow on Father's Days. A decade ago, some of those who lost their dads in Vietnam organized a group called "Sons and Daughters In Touch." It has grown to include more than 3,000 members. They quickly learned that they shared a unique bond.

This is their fourth Father's Day gathering at The Wall. The last was in 1997. About 1,000 sons, daughters, grandchildren and widows are expected for a long weekend of reunion and remembrance. They will be joined by Vietnam veterans to provide answers to lingering questions of "What was my daddy like?"

~

Nearing his thirty-fourth birthday, Sergeant First Class Marshall Robertson was like a father to the eighteen and nineteen year olds who made up his infantry platoon. But after leading them for months, his combat tour was ending. He was pulled out of the boonies in late August of 1969. Then word came to the base camp that the platoon leader, an experienced officer, had been medevacked out. A green lieutenant would be taking the platoon into a hell called Que Son Valley.

Before boarding the chopper back to battle, the platoon sergeant wrote his wife to explain why he had volunteered to return.

"My dear darling ...

"Sometimes a man just has to do what he must. Please forgive me for this but my men have a brand new officer. I just have to go out there and help them out. I know that you will not understand but try to see my side of it ...My love, if I should die over here, it will not be for my country or this country but it will be for my boys ...

"Tell the kiddies that I love them and, if this is my last letter, please remember me."

The Robertson kiddies were aged ten, nine, seven and six when the word came that their dad had been killed in combat while with his platoon. The Army mailed a monthly widow's check to the twenty-nine-year-old woman faced with raising four children alone. But the Army sent no psychologists to help the family handle the grief.

Anti-war sentiment was growing across the country. The Robertson family felt isolated. The message they perceived: "Your dad is dead. Bury him and go on."

Two decades would pass before they read of their father's heroism in his final battle in "Death Valley," a book by Keith William Nolan.

Patricia Wilson, the second oldest of the Robertson kids, called the author and got the names of men from their dad's platoon.

Not knowing if he would even remember her father, she phoned that raw, young lieutenant of yore and said "I'm Marshall Robertson's daughter." There was a silence on the other end of the line. Then sobs. "Your father was truly a professional," he told her. For twenty years, he had borne a burden of guilt about the sergeant who died helping him carry out his first mission. The daughter assured him that the family does not blame the survivors.

Patricia Robertson Wilson is an advertising executive in Atlanta now. She and her three siblings and their mother will be at The Wall on Father's Day. And they're bringing the eight grandchildren of SFC Robertson.

"Growing up, Father's Day was very, very sad for us," she said. "But this is going to be a celebration."

They will celebrate the life of their dad. And they will remember him.

$\sim$

Mickey Olmstead was only five in 1965 when the anti-aircraft flak hit his father's F4B Phantom fighter jet in the sky just south on Hanoi. The impact momentarily knocked out Porter Halyburton, the navigator. When he opened his eyes, Halyburton saw that the pilot's flight helmet was off. He repeatedly called on the intercom and got no response. He figured that Stanley Olmstead had been killed at the age of thirty-one.

The navigator couldn't fly the plane from the back seat, so he bailed out over North Vietnam. The Phantom flew on until it crashed into a mountainside.

An attorney now in Austin, Mickey Olmstead can remember fishing with his dad. He remembers getting a spanking for hitting his little sister, who was two years younger. He remembers going with his dad to the hangers at a naval air station. He remembers "lots of stuff."

For five years after Navy Lieutenant Olmstead's jet was hit, the pilot and navigator were listed as Killed in Action. No one had seen a chute open. But in 1970, word came out of Hanoi that Lieutenant Halyburton was a prisoner of war. So both pilot and navigator were reclassified as Missing in Action and presumed captured. Porter Halyburton was among the POWs who came home at the end of the war. Stanley Olmstead never came home.

"When I was growing up, all the other kids had fathers," recalls Mickey Olmstead. "I felt extremely different and envious."

Over the years, he learned a lot about his dad. Shortly after his engagement to be married, the young Navy pilot had been invited to join the Blue Angels. But he turned down the assignment because it would have kept him away from his bride. The elder Olmstead had been a test pilot. He had been accepted into NASA's astronaut training program upon completion of his tour flying combat missions from the USS Independence, a carrier anchored off the coast of Southeast Asia.

This will be Mickey Olmstead's fourth Father's Day at The Wall. It has helped to be with others who shared the same experiences growing up and to talk with Vietnam vets. He spent the better part of a day with Porter Halyburton during one reunion. The former navigator thinks the pilot died in his plane.

A joint task force on MIAs is searching a mountainside in North Vietnam for the crash site of his dad's fighter. The son says it "would help a great deal" if they could find it.

∼

Growing up in Tampa, Ken Mobley never knew any other kids whose dads had been killed in Vietnam. And he never talked about his own father, Army Chief Warrant Officer Warren H. Mobley, who died in an accidental plane crash over Can Tho. It was one of those strange things that happen in war. His dad was a crew chief flying in a small, fixed wing plane when it collided in mid-air with a South Vietnamese army helicopter on November 24, 1970.

When it happened, Ken Mobley was ten. His brother was six. Afterward, their childhood Father's Days were endured, never enjoyed.

But that was before he started coming to The Wall. He has been to all the Father's Day reunions of Sons and Daughters In Touch. "It was amazing to suddenly meet this group of people who had so much in common," he explains. "It's a unique group."

Often they gather into small "sharing circles," a dozen or so sons and daughters guided by a counselor and perhaps a Vietnam vet. Emotions pent up inside them during a childhood of repressed grief and anger are sometimes released as they share feelings known only to those whose fathers never came home from Vietnam.

The faces behind the names on The Wall are forever young. Increasingly, their offspring are older. It has been twenty-five years since the fall of Saigon.

CWO Mobley was thirty-two when he died. So all though his own life, Ken Mobley would compare his milestones with those of his dad. But when the son turned thirty-three, the comparisons ended. "There was no more road map," he recalls. "It was a real wake-up call."

He is a husband and dad himself, now. He sells automotive classified advertising for the Tampa Tribune. His wife, Rita, and daughters Ilana, nine, and Sarah, four, will be with him at The Wall on Sunday.

After all, it's Father's Day.

Big Rigs and Roses

Daylight was fading over the still Mississippi pastures as Hal T. Burks steered his eighteen-wheeler down Highway 78 toward Tupelo and reflected on the two great loves of his life.

"My pretty wife's name was Demetra," he said. "One time early in our marriage, I had just gotten home from two weeks on the road when the doorbell rang and she got a delivery of roses. There was a card that said 'To Demetra With Love' but no signature."

After some chit-chat about other matters, his wife asked flat-out if he wasn't curious about who sent the flowers.

"I said, 'No. Should I be?' Well, she thought I ought to," Burks recalled. "She had sent them to herself to make me jealous. We laughed about those roses for years. That was the only time she ever tried to get me to quit driving. She knew how much I loved it."

Hal T. and Demetra had been married for twenty-four years and had reared three children to adulthood when she died in 1997 of complications from a liver disease. "I'd been planning to retire when I was fifty-five to be with her," said the fifty-year-old long-haul driver. "Now I'll just keep on trucking."

Many motorists—"four-wheelers" in the lingo of Citizens' Band radio—wonder about the nation's 3.75 million commercial truck drivers like Burks. Romanticized in songs like "Six Days on the Road" and "Eighteen Wheels and a Dozen Roses," they are often portrayed as cow-boys of the interstates. But highway safety activists sometimes depict the drivers as tatooed death on wheels—fatigued or drugged-out renegades speeding 80,000 pounds of jeopardy down the highway.

Riding with Burks through five Southern states, though, the stereotypes vaporize like the exhaust from his white Freightliner. He drinks more bottled water than coffee, for instance, and listens to books on tape as much as to country music radio and CB gab. As for recreation on the road, he said, "give me more than a twelve-hour break and I'll find a golf course."

From his M. S. Carriers headquarters in Memphis to truckstops across America, folks call him "Hal T." His truck has his name on the door, ten forward gears, a 430-horsepower engine and a roomy cab with a refrigerator and bunk beds. It gets about six miles to the gallon of diesel fuel. There's also a company-installed engine governor that restricts his speed to a maximum of sixty-five miles per hour and a Quaalcom satellite hook-up that lets his dispatcher track him—within twenty feet—anywhere on the continent. The system permits instanteous two-way communications through a computer on his dashboard.

Burks is hardly a typical trucker. Over the past two decades or so, he has driven 2.8 million miles—that's five trips to the moon and back—without having an accident. In 1997, the American Trucking Association—which represents most of the major carriers—selected him as an America's Road Team Captain. These dozen drivers are picked because of their performance test scores, safety record and flair for public relations. They represent the trucking industry for 18 months and then a new team is chosen.

～

Driving east on I-20 through the Alabama night, Hal T. Burks shifted gears and spun his stories.

The "T." stands for Travis. He was one of fourteen children born in a farm family outside of Memphis. "I never heard my parents argue," he marveled. Whenever there were differences, "they'd go park by a cornfield and have what Mama called 'loud reasoning'."

One of his schoolmates was the sister of Jerry Lee Lewis and he regularly visited the Killer's Memphis home during his boyhood. He dropped out of high school in the twelfth grade. "My downfall was my

'59 Ford convertible—black with red trim interior," he recalled. "I couldn't stand to sit in class and see that car sitting in the parking lot."

Shortly after leaving school, though, he was driving an olive green "deuce-and-a-half"—a 2.5 ton military truck. He earned a high school equivalency diploma in the Army and served a tour in Vietnam. After his discharge, he was working at a Jackson, Tenn., truckstop owned by his sister and brother-in-law when struck by a yearning to drive a big truck down the road. Since then, he's hauled cargo through 48 states—all but Alaska and Hawaii.

"I like driving anytime," he declared. "And it's great to wake up in a different place every morning."

It was close to midnight when he backed his trailer up to a loading dock at a warehouse in Diluth, Georgia, filled in his log book, and settled into the lower bunk to sleep.

Federal transportation law lets truckers drive for ten straight hours, but then forces them to take an eight-hour break before starting again. Practically every minute is chronicled in the log book, and the Quaalcom system provides computerized documentation.

Paychecks are determined by mileage. Long-distance drivers like Burks who operate company trucks usually earn between 28¢ and 35¢ per mile. Drivers who use their own rigs to haul company cargoes earn more per mile, but also must pay for gas and upkeep of their trucks. The average truck driver makes $35,000 a year, according to the American Trucking Association.

To keep their expenses down and maximize their mileage, drivers usually sleep their eight hours in the cabs rather than in motels. They park in truckstop lots or roadside rest stops or, if possible, at the destination for their cargo. Drivers typically stay on the road for two-week stretches—finding out where to pick up and take the next load only after dropping off the previous one.

Around 8:00 A.M., Burks notified his dispatcher that the Diluth cargo of huge spools of wire had been unloaded. Shortly afterward, a message popped up on the computer screen to pick up a loaded trailer at the M. S. Carriers depot in Atlanta and drive it to Orlando. After hash browns, eggs and sausage at a Waffle House, he drove to the depot where the empty trailer was switched with a full one. The Freightliner was soon headed south on I-75.

Passing miles of piney woods and palmettos, Burks allowed that the road can get lonely. For years, he called his wife and kids every day that he was away.

Separations from family "are the main reasons that a lot of drivers quit," he said. "You can't sit home and make money in the trucking business. It takes a good woman to put up with a trucker. She has got to be it all—plumber, carpenter, sometimes mama and daddy. Most of them can't handle all that."

Although there are increasingly more women behind the wheel, more than nine of every ten long-distance drivers are male.

Burks looks back fondly on an 18-month period when he drove his own rig. "I took my pretty wife with me on the road," he recalled. "We had a great time. But I didn't like spending my days off working on my truck."

Now M. S. Carriers provides him a new truck every couple of years and maintains the vehicles religiously. A new Freightliner costs $80,000 to $100,000 and the Memphis-based carrier has about 2,500 on the road. A trailer costs another $20,000 or so. In addition to its own rigs, M. S. Carriers contracts with 700 to 800 owner-operators. There are a few bigger carriers, but not many.

The trucking business is booming. The industry employs about 9 million people—including 3 million drivers—and there is a national shortage of 80,000 drivers, according to the American Trucking Association. About eighty-two percent of the nation's freight revenue goes to trucking firms and the business has grown by twenty percent over the past decade.

∼

Burks faced an hour-long wait for a shower at the TA Truckstop near the intersection of I-75 and the Florida Turnpike near Wildwood, but wait he would. A day and a half had passed since he left his home in Humbolt, Tenn., and driven to company headquarters in Memphis to begin this two-week run. It was time to clean up and change clothes.

The shower was free with a $50 fuel purchase or $6 without. Truckers got a clean blue towel and matching washcloth and a key to a private tiled bathroom with shower stall, laboratory and toilet. The hot water was welcome.

"There's always a wait in the evening" as truckers fill the parking lots for the night, explained Burks. "The best time to get a shower at a truck-stop is early in the mornings."

But this day's drive has not yet ended. After the shower and a supper of liver and onions, he was back behind the wheel—heading east on the Turnpike to Orlando. Time spent at truckstops doesn't count against the ten-hour driving limit.

Burks' CB handle is "Double Trouble" but he listens more than talks in the conversations that crackle over the airwaves. One night, though, he talked to the driver of Dolly Parton's tour bus. "He told me to look at his back window when he passed," Burks said. "There was ol' Dolly waving at me. Sometimes you'll see country music singers and their crews eating in truckstops in the middle of the night."

It's not just the food and sassy waitresses that pull truckers—and bands' tour buses—to truckstops, but also the huge parking lots and twenty-four-hour services. It's hard to pull a big-rig up to a McDonald's drive-in window.

The streets of Orlando are nearly deserted as the Freightliner arrives around 11:00 P.M. Burks follows the directions on his Quaalcom computer screen to find his destination warehouse. He backs up to a loading dock, enters the time in his log book, and is quickly asleep in the bunk. He is awakened at 6:00 A.M. by a banging on the cab door. A warehouse supervisor told him to move to another bay to be unloaded immediately. Wiping the sleep from his eyes, he complied.

The supervisor pointed to a room with coffee and an adjoining bathroom where drivers can wash their faces and brush their teeth.

Before 8:00 A.M., the trailer was empty and Burks sent the news to his dispatcher. Minutes later came orders to pick up a load about fifty miles away and drive it to Greensboro, North Carolina. Often Burks does not know what he is hauling. A load is a load. And a driver can't make money in a parked truck. Breakfast will come somewhere down the road.

Hal T. Burks was rolling again.

Good Ol' Boys Like Me

The late summer sun was scorching a nearly deserted campus and Pat Dye, the football coach, squinted as he posed with tow- headed children while their pleased parents fired away with Instamatics.

It was picture day for the Auburn Tigers, an easy afternoon for all. So Dye looked at me hard when I asked him, "Coach, how come y'all planted a hedge?" I motioned toward the young shrubs that now surround the field at Jordan-Hare Stadium.

"We ain't copying Georgia so don't write that," Dye replied. "Anyway, ours has stickers."

It suddenly occurred to me that Pat Dye was born and bred for a place like this, a small Southern town where he can rear a family and do his life's work and try to change those things he figures need changing. It also occurred to me that I might belong someplace like that, too.

I work in Washington, D.C., and live in a Virginia suburb. Ambition led me there, I reckon. And ego, too. I used to live in Atlanta. But that never seemed like home, either.

I migrated farther north than most, but there are a lot of folks like me in the boom cities of the Sun Belt. Atlanta. Orlando. Birmingham. Dallas. Folks who were born and raised in small Southern towns; folks who left when they grew up and had to make a living.

That's the reality of the "two Souths" that economists and sociologists have discovered. Folks flock to the cities because there's nothing for them where they left. Nothing that they can spend, anyhow.

I've been in Washington about four years now, long enough to feel like an observer when I spent a week recently driving the back roads of Georgia, Alabama and Florida on an assignment. What I saw, heard and tasted, though, set off longings that hide within a lot of us converted Dixie urbanites.

On a Saturday night, at a motel restaurant in LaGrange, Georgia, the Greenville High School Class of 1943 was celebrating its forty-third reunion. The attending class members and their spouses were assembled around a long table. A waiter seated me within earshot.

One by one, the white-haired class members related the most significant things that had happened to them during the preceeding year. One lady told how she had rushed to the hospital, fearing she was having a heart attack. But the pain was most likely indigestion, she told her former classmates. She blamed it on a mess of turnip greens she had eaten, along with some corn bread and pepper sauce.

"If my husband ever eats turnip greens again," she vowed, "it won't be at my table."

Another class member had retired that year and learned, with some disappointment, that "the railroad yard runs without me." One couple had gone to the Kentucky Derby. A widow's boyfriend had married somebody else. When a missing classmate's name was mentioned, it was revealed in hushed tones that "he's had a drinking problem." The consensus was that nobody at Greenville High forty-three years ago ever would have expected it.

By 10:00 P.M., the reunion had broken up. Many of the class still live around Meriwether County, anyway, and would see each other in church the following morning.

I had roots like that once, back when I was a barefoot boy in Brunswick, Georgia, running through a sandy park named for my great-great grandfather. A stained glass window at our Methodist church had the names of my ancestors etched on it. My grandmother lived right behind us. I could run from our house to her's before the screen door on our back porch slammed shut. I did it a lot.

My granddaddy on the other side lived on a farm, about a two-hour's drive away. We would spend weeks there in the summers. Go fishing in the pond. Swing on the front porch. Watch them work in the cotton fields and tobacco barns. Looking back, my granddaddy probably knew I was lazy. But he loved me anyway and let me ride in the back of his truck to see the monkey at Sinclair's Grocery in Snipesville.

My children have been to a picnic on the White House lawn. They go to the Capitol and talk to congressmen and visit the Smithsonian right regularly. They take lessons in ballet and karate and French and computers and all kinds of stuff. But the only time they go barefoot is at the swimming pool. And they only see their grandparents once or twice a year, for a week or so. They don't really know each other that well.

As I watched and listened to those good people at the class reunion in LaGrange, I wondered how often they got to see their grandchildren.

We all just do the best we can, I guess.

A couple of days later, I drove from Auburn down to Tallahassee, Florida. Much of the way, I listened to a country music station out of Alexander City, Alabama. I always wish I could write lines like some in country songs. Lines like "living my life like I had something better to do." That pretty well sums up certain periods of my existence.

Anyway, I stopped at a place in Lumpkin, Georgia, for breakfast. Ordered the Sawmill Special: Sausage, two eggs, grits, and two biscuits covered with sawmill gravy. You flat can't eat like that in Washington, D.C. I'd almost forgotten, too, how they automatically refill your iced tea glass in little Southern restaurants and how you have to drive around the courthouse square when you pass through town on the highway.

These are hard times for the rural South. But the people on front porches still wave when a car drives past, and you can still buy boiled peanuts on the side of the road. The crops have dried up, but the "Jesus Saves" signs in the fields still assure the faithful that a better time is coming.

When I got to Tallahassee, I called up a friend named Randy Briley. I don't have many friends. Oh, I've got a lot of colleagues and neighbors and guys to talk about sports with. But only a handful of friends. Randy is a fraternity brother. We were SAEs together. Used to stay up all night drinking beer and guarding the fraternity house lion against painters and growing up. That was nearly twenty years ago. A lot of Southern men, I think, find their friends early and stick with them through life. My daddy goes fishing with a boyhood friend he has been going fishing with for sixty years.

My wife, Sherry, on the other hand, has made good friends everywhere I've dragged her to live.

None of my lifelong friends lives north of South Georgia. I don't know what that signifies. My friend in Tallahassee grew up there, went to college there, and is raising a family there. Some of us find continuity.

We went to Doc's, a bar owned by another old fraternity brother. It's got a basketball goal in the middle where patrons shoot foul shots for beers, kind of like throwing darts in less athletic establishments. We drank too many pitchers of Michelob Light and talked about old times and what has happened to the boys we once were and to other boys and girls we once knew. We talked about wives and children. We talked about football some, but not that much.

Football, especially college football, is important in the South. That's one of the things I miss about living there—the importance of football. But I only see Randy every couple of years or so.

We were late getting to his house, and he hadn't called his wife until the evening was well under way. She was gracious. I rocked their baby in my lap.

We got up the next morning and ran a couple of miles, sweating out the beer of the previous night and reassuring ourselves that we were still jocks. Kind of like in the movie "The Big Chill." I always run with my friends when we haven't seen each other for a long time. Or sometimes we'll play touch football or whiffle ball home run derby. Rituals of friends growing older.

Later, I headed north from Tallahassee, north toward home. My children have Yankee accents. They won't eat grits. I missed them anyway. On the way to the airport, I heard one of my all-time favorite songs.

The chorus goes:

"But I still hear the soft southern wind in the live oak trees

"Those Williams boys still mean a lot to me—Hank and Tennessee

"I guess we're all gonna be what we're gonna be . . ."

Don Williams sings it. The last line is *"What do you do with good ol' boys like me?"*

I wonder.